Now What Do I Do?

Now What Do I Do?

A Guide to Parenting
Elementary-Aged
Children

JULIE A. ROSS, M.A.

St. Martin's Griffin ✻ New York

Design by Ellen R. Sasahara

Library of Congress Cataloging-in-Publication Data

Ross, Julie A.
    Now what do I do? : a guide to parenting elementary-aged children
/ by Julie Ross. — 1st ed.
        p.   cm.
    ISBN 0-312-18208-2
    1. Parenting.   2. Parent and child.   3. Education, Elementary—
Parent participation.   4. Home and school.   I. Title.
    HQ755.8.R6753   1998
649'.124—dc21   97-35513
                                                                                          CIP

First St. Martin's Griffin Edition: March 1998

10   9   8   7   6   5   4   3   2   1

Acknowledgments

Many thanks to my daughter, Emilie, and my son, Daniel. I'm grateful for their steadfast love and extreme patience in the moments when I, too, struggle with being a better parent. Along with my husband, Steve, they are my greatest treasures.

I'm also grateful to Steve, whose enthusiastic whoops and hollers upon the completion of each of my books are only matched by his excitement when I begin a new project. His encouragement, love, and devotion keep me going.

Thanks to my mother, Kim Yerly, who took the time to read the book cover to cover prior to submission and give her editorial viewpoint and sage advice.

I'd also like to thank my agent, Rita Rosenkranz. I'm grateful for both her hands-on style and her enthusiastic encouragement throughout this process.

Many thanks once again, to my editor, Jennifer Weis, who believes in the value of getting practical advice out to parents, who are so often desperately in need of solutions rather than theory. Thanks also to Linda Price, who talked me through the editorial changes and whose enthusiastic response to the book brightened my day.

Finally, I'd like to thank the members of my workshops. Their stories, their joys, their frustrations, and their sorrows about child rearing make my writing an easier task. It is they who are pictured within these pages. The techniques and tools that you will read about are parent tested, because my group members trusted me enough to take the techniques home and work with them—sometimes at great length. Their ability to trust, to try, and sometimes to fail has made this an honest book.

Contents

Part Three: Your Child's World

Now What Do I Do?

Introduction

Congratulations! You made it. You and your child survived the toddler years. He's finally toilet trained and she gave up the bottle even though you thought it might never happen. There seem to be fewer tantrums, and most of the time your children are more cooperative. Everyone's in school all day and asleep all night. It's a miracle!

Then the phone rings. It's your neighbor. "I hate to be the one to tell you this, but your child has been, well, taking things from my child and hiding them in his backpack." Taking things? As in stealing? You confront your child. "Did you take something from our neighbor?" Your child vehemently denies it, calls the neighbor a liar, says the other child "gave" him the item, then storms off and slams the door to his room. Now what do you do?

Or maybe one day your child comes home from school and says, "I hate school, I'm never going back. And I'm not doing my homework either." You beg, you plead, you promise rewards, you threaten punishment. Maybe you even carry through on the punishment. Nothing. She clams up and won't talk about it. The next morning you have to physically drag her from the house, kicking and screaming. At the end of the day, her attitude is worse. Now what do you do?

Perhaps it's that your child is being rude, calling you names, using four-letter words in front of her grandparents. Maybe life has suddenly become a never-ending power struggle. Maybe your son wants to know what "sex" means. Perhaps your daughter is afraid to sleep in her own bed at night. And you think to yourself "Now what do I do?"

1

Elementary school marks the beginning of a new chapter in your child's life and a new chapter in parenting. The issues that come up for our children during these years, the questions they ask, the limits they test, and how we handle these matters directly affect how they will handle adolescence and the years beyond.

Once adolescence arrives, it will test not only our strength as parents but our children's strength as people. At that point, they will begin to question their sense of self, put both your and their own values to the test, make independent decisions that may affect the rest of their lives. How our children handle the difficulties of adolescence depends on how strong a "root system" we help them establish during elementary school. Without strong roots, our young "saplings" stand the chance of being blown over during the stormy adolescent years.

The root system we nurture during elementary school has many branches. During this time, our children are given new responsibilities. They're expected to handle school both socially and academically. They're required to do chores and take on new responsibilities at home. How we support them in handling these responsibilities will measure their success in school and society later on.

Our children are going to have new questions about the way the world works. They will be curious about sexuality, violence, relationships, why people behave the way they do. How we answer these questions is integral to the development of their value system—the very system they'll have to rely on during adolescence.

New behaviors will emerge. Our children may lie or steal or cheat for the first time in their lives. The balance between enforcing consequences for their actions and creating an atmosphere that allows them to tell us the truth is a delicate one. If done well, it preserves the parent-child relationship and teaches the lesson at the same time.

To resist the negative peer pressure so prevalent in junior high and high school, children must have developed a strong sense of self already. Learning to listen without judgment, communicating understanding of a child's negative as well as positive feelings, and handling our own feelings during our children's elementary school years helps build our children's self-esteem and teaches them to listen to their inner voice when faced with decisions about right and wrong.

The creation and enforcement of rules, and likewise our ability to expand those rules as our children progress through elementary school, determine whether they will become responsible people and learn to problem-solve in a mature way.

Throughout this book, I talk about giving children the resources to handle the many situations that arise for them. Resources are the internalized information and/or emotional strength that our children can draw on in making decisions, taking responsibility, and handling their feelings. Children's informational resources come from many places: how they've successfully solved problems in the past; what their family's values are; how they've seen parents, peers, and others successfully handle problem solving. Children need emotional resources as well. These are the resources that come from feeling unconditionally loved and supported in their home environment. Emotional resources help our children handle difficult social and relationship issues that arise for them during the day. These resources develop from a nurturing, strong family unit. Practical guidelines for giving children informational as well as emotional resources are discussed throughout this book.

This book translates theory into practical technique. I've read far too many books that infused me with guilt and worry about my parenting. These books told me what I was doing wrong and that I should be doing things differently, but never seemed to answer the question of *how* to handle a particular situation more constructively. This book gives you tools, scripts, and practical solutions to common problems. It talks about the specific situations most commonly faced by the parent of an elementary school child. Each chapter contains proven techniques that not only teach you *how* to handle the situation but ensure that you remain connected with your child and that you establish and strengthen his root system, his resources, and your relationship in the process. You'll gain the most benefit from reading the whole book. Even if a particular problem doesn't apply to you, the techniques contained within each chapter build on those given in previous chapters, and each technique can be used in many different situations.

The elementary school years can be the most pleasurable ones we will spend with our children. It is a time when they can be the most flexible, the easiest to talk to, and the most willing to listen to what we have to say. We have a once-in-a-lifetime opportunity during these years to solidify our relationship with our children, lay the foundation in both discipline and communication for the years to come, and build and strengthen our children's self-esteem in the process. While the pleasure of our children during these years lends itself to a more relaxed attitude about child rearing, we must keep in mind that being relaxed doesn't mean that we stop thinking. The critical groundwork for the turbulent teens is laid during these years. Let's take advantage of the opportunity!

Part One

Your Child's Day

Chapter 1

"It's Impossible to Get My Child Out in the Morning!"

Many nutritionists tell us that breakfast is the most important meal of the day. After a long night's fast, we need to refuel, to stock up on important nutrients in order for our bodies and our minds to be alert and ready for the long day ahead.

Psychologically as well, our children need the opportunity to begin each day afresh, gathering their resources and feeling emotionally fed by our interactions with them in the morning. Yet for many parents, mornings are a disaster! The "Have a nice day" that we call to our children as they go through those school doors often means "Thank God they're out of my hair!"

"Mornings are the worst! Everyone's tense, my children are slower than molasses, and half the time my husband and I get into an argument as well. No one can find their homework from the night before, breakfast is a short-order cook's worst nightmare, and frankly, I've had it. Sometimes I scream and yell, but that only seems to make things worse. I'm at my wit's end."

Ever feel like this mom? I think we all have.

With this kind of a beginning, children use up some of the resources they need as they enter their school day. For them to handle the social, educational, and emotional issues that arise at school, in an effective way, they must begin with all of their resources intact.

Difficult Beginnings

"It's simply a matter of my son's dawdling. I'm convinced that if he would just pick up his feet in the morning and get moving, without being so distracted by the things around him, then we'd make it to school on time. But every day it's the same thing. I get him out of bed at seven and tell him to get dressed. Then I take my shower, but when I go back into his room at seven-fifteen, he hasn't even started. At that point, I start to feel tense. I tell him again to get dressed, but I can't stay and monitor him, because I have to get ready too. By seven-thirty, he may have on his pants and one sock. He still hasn't eaten breakfast, his homework is in five different places, and he hasn't combed his hair. We always get into an argument about breakfast too. I start yelling, he yells back at me, and I end up putting his shoes on him and combing his hair as he's eating as well as getting his homework and school things together myself."

This mom is caught in a negative routine with her son, and it's clearly making the beginning of the day difficult for both mother and child.

The Importance of Routines

As human beings, we thrive on routines. They enable us to be efficient about getting to work on time in the morning, they allow us to get our jobs (in and out of the home) done satisfactorily, they help us wind down at the end of the day. Routines make our daily lives feel familiar and comfortable. They lessen tension because we no longer have to "think on our feet" as we go along; with a routine we know what to expect.

Through experience, most adults have come to view the world

as fairly predictable. We have fallen into routines as a matter of course rather than choice. For most children between the ages of five and ten years, the world is still a highly unpredictable place where they have little or no control over the events that happen to them. Implementing a positive morning routine brings order to the chaos.

Positive Routines vs. Negative Routines

A morning routine should consist of four to six clear steps that occur in the same order day after day. For example:

1. Get out of bed.
2. Get dressed.
3. Get homework/school items ready.
4. Eat breakfast.
5. Brush teeth.
6. Read, play, or watch television.

This is an example of a positive routine, but not all routines look like this. Sometimes we unintentionally fall into patterns that might be considered routine but that make for an unpleasant or negative experience. An example of a negative routine might look like this:

1. Nag child to get out of bed.
2. Child gets out of bed.
3. Fight about getting dressed.
4. Get dressed.
5. Try to find misplaced school items.
6. Eat breakfast.
7. Argue over brushing teeth.

One mother told me that day after day she would get her daughter out of bed in the morning, and they would fight about what clothes were appropriate to wear that day. One day the daughter got up and got dressed in appropriate clothing before the mother even came in to her room. Later, at breakfast, her daughter suddenly looked startled and said, "Mom! We forgot our fight today!"

Using a Positive Routine to Motivate Your Child

If you look closely at the example of a positive routine, you'll notice that (with the exception of brushing teeth) the parts of the routine that the child is most likely to resist occur first—getting dressed, getting schoolwork together—and the parts that are the least likely to be a problem occur later—eating breakfast and reading, playing, or watching television. All effective routines must have a component that will motivate your child. To discover that component, ask yourself what your child is currently doing instead of getting ready. Is she playing on her computer? Is he absorbed in Legos? Is she "zoned out" in front of the television? Simply rearrange the order such that what the child *wants* to do in the morning occurs last. This is what we call a work-first, play-later attitude. By ordering the routine so that there are motivating factors toward the end, parents can avail themselves of the opportunity to use the enjoyable parts of the routine to get their child going, as in "When you've gotten dressed and your backpack is ready, then you can have breakfast," or "When you've brushed your teeth, then you can read (play on the computer, watch television)."

Choosing Your Words

"Wait a second! My son has a terrible time eating breakfast. If I say to him 'If you don't get dressed, you can't have breakfast,' he'd just starve himself. We'd never get either one accomplished."

First of all, your choice of words is important. Rather than saying "if," say "when." Children hear "if" as a threat, a challenge to engage in a battle of wills with the parent. It's the rare child who won't meet that challenge head on. "If" also implies that there is an option about getting dressed, which there's not. On the other hand, "when" implies that this is something you expect of your child. It is, in fact, a "positive expectation." Most parents know (or at least have been told) that children live up to our negative expectations. For example, if you call a child a klutz, he'll become a klutz. The same is true of positive expectations. In saying "when you get dressed," the child hears "I expect you to get dressed."

"Okay, let's say I change the wording. I still think my child is going to be willing to give up breakfast. He just doesn't care about it."

This may be true, and if you have a child who's simply not hungry in the morning (or not hungry enough for it to motivate him), then you won't offer that as your motivating factor. Instead, you'll say "When you're finished getting dressed and have your school things together, then you can watch television (or read, or play.)"

What About the Child for Whom Breakfast Is a Problem?

"But what if eating breakfast is the big issue? My daughter gets completely ready, but I can't get her to eat more than a few bites of breakfast. Should I place breakfast first in the routine?"

If getting your child to eat more (or eat less) is a big issue, then your problem goes beyond difficulty with the morning routine. Eating is a bodily function, which should have no more nor less significance than other bodily functions, such as going to the bathroom. Studies indicate that children are excellent judges of how much, when, and what they need to eat in order to stay healthy. Authors such as Jane Hirschmann and Lela Zaphiropoulos in their book *Preventing Childhood Eating Problems* and Ellyn Satter in her book *How to Get Your Kid to Eat . . . But Not Too Much"* emphasize the importance of allowing children to self-regulate—that is, giving them the opportunity to discover what, when, and how much they need to eat in order to feel satisfied. Satter discusses a division of responsibility in the "feeding relationship" between parent and child. The parent has the responsibility of providing nutritious food, the child has the responsibility of deciding whether, or even if, he should eat. Unless you have been told by your pediatrician that your child is ill, has special dietary needs, or is failing to grow, it is my recommendation that eating breakfast be your child's decision and that it never should become a power struggle. If your child chooses not to eat, let him go hungry. He will learn from the natural consequences of getting hungry before lunchtime that it's probably best to eat at least a little something in the morning. Remember that studies indicate that the more you struggle with your child over eating, the worse it will become. Eating disorders among teenagers and adults are on the rise in this country, so if you suspect that the "feeding relationship" with your child is distorted, I suggest you get professional guidance from a therapist so that your child won't end up being one of the statistics.

Enforcing Consequences

"I really feel like we have a good routine—at least in terms of including a 'motivator.' The problem is that it doesn't motivate him! The other day I told him that when he'd finished getting dressed, then he could play with the building he'd made of blocks the day before. I turned my back, and there he was, playing with the building anyway. So I picked up the blocks and put them away."

This father did a great job. He used what we call "logical consequences" when his son disregarded the order of the routine. A logical consequence is the logical result of a child's choice to violate the rules or values that his parents have made clear in the past. It is an action or series of actions that a parent can enforce and that teach a lesson in the process. Because this child was being distracted by the building blocks, Dad took away the distraction. The clear message to the child was twofold: Dad means what he says, and the blocks are not to be played with until the end of the routine.

Logical consequences require a little forethought on a parent's part, because sometimes they're not easy to come up with. The key to effective consequences lies in their logical relationship to the misbehavior or rule violation. In this way, they approximate the natural consequences that exist in the real world and are such powerful teachers. When the consequence of a child's behavior is logically related to the choice she made, it allows her to both internalize the lesson and ultimately generalize to other situations. Therefore, she develops the resources necessary to make good decisions in the future—even when a parent isn't there to guide her. In addition, when a consequence is logically linked to misbehavior, the child may not like it, but it usually resonates with her sense of justice. Therefore, she may yell and scream to see if she can get you to change your mind, but internally, there is an acceptance of the consequence as just or fair.

Coming Up with Logical Consequences

In all the parent groups I've ever taught, the single thing I hear the most is that logical consequences are difficult to come up with. This is true—at least in the beginning. Much like the initial work we must do in an exercise class to strengthen our muscles, working our brain to come up with consequences that are logically related to misbehavior is a struggle in the beginning. But, also like muscles that are strengthened by repeated exercise, coming up with logical consequences becomes easier over time. In order to get you started, if you're having difficulty coming up with a logical consequence for your child's behavior in the morning, ask yourself two things:

1. What is my child doing instead of what he's supposed to do?
2. How is this inconveniencing me?

Looking at #1, Dad assessed that his child was playing with blocks instead of proceeding with the routine. The logical consequence was to take away what the child was doing. If your child is doing something else instead of what he's supposed to do, take it away as the logical consequence.

Now look at #2. Let's say that your child's dawdling is inconveniencing you because it means that you have to get his backpack together to get out of the house on time. The logical consequence would be to leave his backpack home. (Yes, in spite of his protests about the consequences at school.) By not allowing yourself to be inconvenienced, you'll motivate him to take back his responsibility.

When you find yourself struggling with logical consequences (in the morning or any other time for that matter), remember these two questions. And if you can't come up with a logical consequence right off the bat, get through the situation as best you can and think about it during the day. Most children give us repeated opportunities to set appropriate limits!

The Consequences for You

"My daughter was dawdling in the morning, and her room was a mess. I had asked her to please pick it up before school, but it didn't happen. I told her that she could either pick up before school, or she'd have to skip playing at her friend's house after school so she could come home and clean her room. Of course, she didn't listen! But then I was stuck because I needed her to go to her friend's house so I could finish up some work I was doing. I feel like I wound up punishing myself!"

Mom actually created a lovely logical consequence here. The problem, however, is that while the consequence was one she could enforce, and it was logically related to the misbehavior, it wasn't really one *she* could live with because it inconvenienced her too much. When this happens, we either fail to follow through on a consequence (which teaches our children that we don't mean what we say), or we stick with it, but wind up angry and frustrated because we feel punished as well. It's far better to try to choose consequences where the child is the only one who's affected. For example, perhaps Mom could have said that she'd pick up the room and put the things in a large plastic bag, but then her daughter wouldn't be able to have them for a week. Or she might have said that whatever was left lying around on the floor until Saturday would have to be cleaned up then before her daughter could go out to play.

"But what if we can't come up with another consequence? I mean, I hear that we shouldn't wind up punishing ourselves, but isn't it sometimes unavoidable? Or is it better to just have no consequence at all?"

Absolutely not! The truth is that while it's better to come up with consequences that affect only the misbehaving child, sometimes the lesson is just too important to let it slide. Perhaps it will help to remember that as the parent, you are the leader in the family and the teacher to your children. Therefore, there will be occasions when you'll have to experience a little inconvenience in order for your child to learn from the consequences of his actions. If the mother in the last situation felt strongly about the room being clean before school but really couldn't come up with a different consequence, then it's more important for her to follow through and experience some inconvenience herself rather than let it slide. She should remember that her daughter probably will learn a big lesson from this consequence, and it's unlikely that the girl will dawdle during her morning routine again.

Asking for Help

"We used to have a good morning routine, and we always got to school on time. All of a sudden, my daughter started dawdling and resisting getting dressed. I've told her that when she's ready she can watch a little TV, and she used to respond to that, but not anymore. Something changed, but it wasn't the routine."

What changed is the child. From time to time, our children undergo developmental changes. With these changes come new behaviors. Often, when this happens, our children seek more independence or power. At this point, it is appropriate to ask your child to help come up with a different routine in the morning. You might sit down with her and say something like "Seems like you've been having some difficulty getting ready in the morning, and I thought maybe you might have some suggestions for making it easier." One mother who approached her seven-year-old son in this way received this response:

"Okay! I really think that we need a list of things that have to get done. Then we can decide what things we should do at night and what things can be done in the morning."

After this enthusiastic and unexpected response, mother and son sat down and made a list. They decided that if he got his backpack packed the night before and put his socks and shoes by the door, this would lessen the tension in the morning. They agreed that they would post a checklist on his bedroom door, and as he got ready, step by step, he would check off all the items. This helped him maintain focus and eliminated the need for Mom to nag and yell. Taking the time to have a conversation about this, rather than simply issuing commands, helped this family develop a sense of teamwork and cooperation. The son felt respected and important, and he learned something about the value of organization in the process.

Teaching Is Important

I think that many times parents fall into the trap of believing that every issue with their children is a battle of wills, a case of "Us vs. Them." Sometimes it's helpful to remember that what may appear to be a deliberate attempt on your child's part to make your life more difficult is really the result of inexperience. In reviewing your parental role and the responsibilities attached to it, consider that seeing yourself as your child's teacher sometimes can help you avoid these power struggles.

When we sit down with our children and engage them in a discussion about how to solve a situation that is proving to be difficult for the family in some way, we are giving them the opportunity to learn something about the way families work, teaching them problem-solving and decision-making skills, and helping them develop a sense of individual as well as familial responsibility.

Teaching Doesn't Mean Lecturing

This doesn't mean that we have license to launch into a full-blown lecture. Lecturing rarely works well with anyone, except perhaps college students (and then only for the highly motivated ones). Most educators these days know that in order for children to internalize the lessons they're taught, they must experience the lesson rather than memorize it. This means asking as well as answering their own questions about a subject, working with it in a hands-on manner, and learning to evaluate their own thought processes as they work. Part of my own daughter's third-grade homework each night was to read for half an hour, then write down a question or comment about what she'd read. A quarter of the way into the year she had amassed a large number of comments and questions about the wide variety of books she'd been reading. One night her homework was to read over those questions/comments and write down four or five observations about the patterns she saw that had developed in her thinking.

As parents who are working to teach our children how to grow up, we can use the same philosophies from which our children are benefiting at school.

Asking Questions

Rather than lecturing, ask open-ended questions of your child to get her thinking about the problems that mornings present. Say things like "Can you think of anything we might be able to do about this?" If you have a suggestion yourself, frame it as a question as well. "What do you think about . . . ?" or "What do you think would happen if we tried . . . ?" While at first your child might shrug his shoulders and say "I don't know," eventually this type of teaching—teaching our children how to think—will pay off.

"Our mornings were typically terrible, so I asked my daughter what we could do about the morning routine. At first she shrugged, but I pressed a little further. I told her that it seemed to me that it wasn't just my problem but hers as well. Mornings certainly weren't pleasant for either of us, and she had to agree to that! Finally she suggested that she'd like to get dressed after breakfast rather than before. Well, I hardly thought that would help, but I kept my mouth shut. Instead I told her that I was proud she was able to think of something, and we'd definitely try it and see how it worked. And do you know what? It did work! I couldn't believe it, but suddenly she was cooperative and helpful again!"

When children come up with a solution to a problem, they're more likely to internalize it and follow through.

The Child Who Won't Talk About It

"My son doesn't delay during the routine, he simply won't get out of bed at all! I've tried to catch him at another time to discuss what would make it easier for him to get out of bed, but he won't talk about it. All he does is jump up and down and get wild."

For a child who simply won't get up in the morning, it's always best to attempt to engage his cooperation. That way you won't find yourself resorting to trying to pull him out of bed physically. Sometimes, though, as in this mother's case, children believe that if they don't listen, they won't have to listen. The boy's jumping around and being wild is an attempt to distract Mom from the issue at hand and an effort to get away with not having to listen or engage cooperatively in general. Before sitting down with her child to talk about the problem, this parent needs to have a list of consequences that she will follow through on automatically if her son still refuses to engage with her. This might include going to bed an hour earlier to make it easier to get up in the morning, buying a loud alarm clock and setting it to go off thirty minutes before the child has to get out of bed (in a place he can't reach to turn it off), and setting out an extra set of clothes near the front door, so if he's really late, he can step out in his pajamas and get dressed on the way to school. Armed with these options, Mom can then approach her son again, saying "I'd like to sit down and talk with you about what will make it easier for you to get up in the morning." When he refuses (which of course he will do), she then can say "Well, if you'd like to help come up with a plan, I'd be happy to hear it. But if not, I've thought of the things that I'm going to do to help motivate you. You will go to bed an hour earlier, an alarm will sound thirty minutes prior to the time you need to get up, and I'll put some clothes by the door, so that you can get dressed on the way to school if we start running too late for you to get dressed here. Would you like to have some input, or shall we just move ahead with my plan?" Most children will choose to have some input because they dislike being deprived of their power. Mom's real message here is "This is going to happen, and either I can control it, or you can."

Respect Is Important

In order for children to "hear" what we say to them with the least amount of rebellion, it's important that they not feel attacked. Sometimes parents yell and scream at their children in an effort to promote listening. Robert Fulghum, in his book *All I Really Need to Know I Learned in Kindergarten,* tells a story about a culture that, when the members need to cut down a tree that's too big to be felled with an ax, will send a tribesman with special powers to go out every morning to yell at the tree. After thirty days, the tree dies and falls over. According to the natives, yelling at the tree kills its spirit.

When we yell at our children on a regular basis, we attack the core of their being—their spirit. Children who are attacked in this way feel a need to defend themselves. Sometimes they'll defend their spirit by passively or actively rebelling, sometimes by yelling back. Sometimes their spirit just dies, like the trees the natives scream at.

Using a respectful tone of voice, even when you discipline, not only preserves your child's spirit but will win his respect as well.

Sometimes Things Get Worse Before They Get Better

It's important to realize that when you begin to change your child's routine in the morning, to engage her cooperation, and ultimately to use discipline when it's called for, your child's behavior might get worse before it gets better. Most children will go through a phase of "testing" to see if the new routine or the new limits are going to be firm. Children test us because it is one of the ways they learn about the world and their relationship to it. From the beginning of his life, your child has learned about the world through exploration, manipulation, and experimentation. By putting objects in her mouth during infancy, she learns what they taste and feel like as well as how others feel about her actions. By testing your new firm routine and guidelines for maintaining that routine, she will learn what it feels like to have Mom or Dad lovingly support her in adhering to the values the family has about interacting with each other as well as being to places on time. This exploration of limits will lead to an internalization of your values.

Chapter 2
School Days, School Days, Dear Old Golden Rule Days . . .

Transitioning to School

Whether your child is going into "big school" (kindergarten) for the first time or simply going back to school after a summer vacation, this transition almost always involves a certain amount of anxiety. As adults, the transition from summertime to school time seems relatively easy. After all, the date for the beginning of school probably has been part of your planning for the summer—you had to keep it in mind to plan vacations, make alternate child care arrangements during that time, buy school supplies and clothing for the fall. For children, however, the days flow endlessly one into the other and summertime is eternal. Thus, as school approaches in the fall, it is important that we, as parents, provide an opportunity for our children to make the transition with as little stress and anxiety as possible.

The Importance of Rituals

Engaging your child in some sort of ritual prior to the beginning of school is extremely helpful. Taking her to shop for new school clothes and supplies, for example, will enable her to make the mental leap from the lazy days of summer to the more structured days of fall. One father and son developed the following ritual.

"My son and I have a date the week before school starts every year. We go to the movies, then out for lunch or an early dinner. It began when he was entering kindergarten for the first time, and I saw that he was a little nervous. I just wanted some time to let him air his feelings, but one thing led to another, and we wound up with what's now our 'annual end-of-summer date.' I thought that as he got older, he might find it embarrassing to have a date with Dad, but he really seems to look forward to it every year."

Children do look forward to the traditions that we establish, as long as they're *fun*. If shopping for school clothes is a chore, then for heaven's sake, don't make that your ritual. Choose something that both you and your child can look forward to with pleasure.

Your Attitude Is Important

Equally important to the ritual you set up to ease the transition back to school is your attitude about school, your communication with your child about the upcoming transition, your perceptiveness with regard to her feelings about school, and your ability to give her a measure of control when she's feeling overwhelmed or anxious.

As parents, we have the unique opportunity to influence our children's attitudes, beliefs, values, and self-esteem. For children to succeed—not only in school but in all areas of their lives—parents must project a positive, encouraging attitude.

Yet this isn't always easy, especially if your own experience with school was less than enjoyable.

"I hated school. I was an average student, looked like a geek, and never really felt I fit in. I was always the biggest in my class, so everyone made fun of me. It seemed like I just didn't excel at anything. I can't help cringing inside each year when my daughter talks about going back to school. Part of me prays that she won't have the same experience I did, but another part of me anticipates that she will."

If you had a poor experience in school, it's important not to let your experience serve as a self-fulfilling prophecy for your child. While you may not have enjoyed school, there's no reason why your child shouldn't. Even if your child looks like you or has similar difficulties with certain subjects, there's no reason to think that he'll have the same experience. For one thing, your child is a unique individual, and while some aspects of his personality or learning style or looks may seem similar, it is the things that are different that will create a different experience for him. Likewise, the world has changed considerably since you were a child. That's not to say that children aren't still cruel to other children at times, but the other individuals with whom your child attends school plus your child's teacher and the philosophy of the school will all factor into the unique dynamic your child experiences.

Set Your Child Up for Success

Despite your willingness to put aside your own feelings about school, you still may unwittingly convey your feelings about it to your child unless you take specific steps to set both you and your child up for success.

Don't Joke

Joking around is a technique some parents employ when they feel uncomfortable with a particular subject. Humor certainly has its place in parenting. The problem is that when you feel uncomfortable and use humor to "lighten" the situation, those feelings of discomfort often come through anyway. Instead of a "joke," it comes across as sarcasm. Children don't get the subtle jokes inherent in sarcasm. For example, if you say to your child in a teasing tone of voice: "Soon school will be here and it'll be time to buckle down. No more lazing around for you!" you will send the strong message that school is something to be anxious about, that it means you have to work *with no play,* that it is something to be "gotten through" until next summer when things will be easier. While an adult would laugh and probably respond with another joke, children take things at face value. This is no joke to a child. As adults, we must find ways to be good role models for our children. If this means examining our own feelings about school and even suppressing them to some degree in order to encourage our children to do well, then that is part of our parental responsibilities.

Communication Is the Key

Another way in which we set our children up to succeed in school is by actively maintaining open lines of communication. This is easier said than done. Many of us unwittingly block communication even when we act with good intentions. We want our children to feel comfortable with the idea of going to school, so we offer advice, make suggestions, distract them with the "good" things about school, and so on . . . all in order to comfort them. In reality, however, these "techniques" only serve to communicate to our children that we don't understand how they feel and that perhaps they should keep their anxiety to themselves instead of talking about it. Even what we might consider preventive communication can be potentially harmful.

"My daughter came to me about two weeks before school started and told me she was a little nervous about going back. I didn't

want her to feel nervous, because I remember feeling that way myself and I really think it colored my attitude about school throughout the year. So I told her that there was no reason to feel nervous. I tried to remind her of what a good year she had last year, and told her she'd be with all her friends, and wouldn't that be nice? It was almost like I could see her eyes glaze over in the middle of my "speech," and when I paused, she changed the subject and told me she had to go to her room to call a friend. I guess I said something wrong, but what?"

This mother, like many of us, had entirely good intentions when she gave this "speech." Her desire, entirely honorable, was to help her daughter through her nervousness by reminding her about the positive aspects of school and giving her something to look forward to (seeing her friends). Unfortunately, many times our children don't actually hear our good intentions.

What We Say May Not Be What They Hear

We've all had the experience of becoming entangled in an argument with another human being. And I think many times we wonder, in the middle of that argument, how on earth we wound up arguing. Sometimes it may even seem as if both you and the person you're arguing with have the exact same point of view, yet the fight is continuing. This happens because often what we say is not necessarily what someone else hears us say. Several components make up good communication: clarity on the part of the speaker, a willingness to hear on the part of the listener, a respectful tone of voice. But there's something else too. I can only describe it as a "like mind-set." For example, if your spouse has had a crummy day at work but you've had a terrific day at work, then when you meet at the end of the day, your mind-sets are likely to be different. This difference in mind-sets will affect your communication.

"The other day when my husband, Frank, came home, I was in a great mood. The kids had been delightful all day, and I felt calm and relaxed. We did our normal nighttime ritual, and I thought the kids were being terrific. Oh, there were a few moans of 'Why do we have to go to bed now?' and 'Can't we just watch one more show on TV?' but nothing out of the ordinary. When they finally got in bed, and Frank and I were alone, he said, 'God, those kids are such work.' Well, I suddenly felt this rush of anger toward Frank that surprised me. So, on edge, I said, 'What are you talking about, they're terrific kids.' He countered with 'I didn't say they weren't terrific, just that they're a lot of work.' 'It's the same thing!' I told him. 'No, it's not,' he replied. And we got in this huge argument about it. Later, when we'd both calmed down a little, I realized that we had been coming from two different mind-sets. At the end of his long and, it turned out, stressful day at work, the kids felt overwhelming to him. I, on the other hand, was coming from a more relaxed place. So while Frank said 'those kids are work,' what I heard was 'they're terrible kids.' Taking that one step further, I probably also assumed that he was regretting our decision to have them at all."

If different mind-sets between adults result in arguments and miscommunication, it's not difficult to see why parents and children sometimes have difficulty communicating. Parents and children operate from two entirely different developmental levels. Their agendas are different, as are their priorities and the significance they place on the events that happen to them. For example, when a child drops an ice cream cone and begins to cry, it may be difficult for a parent to understand the tears. After all, with our greater experience we know that it's easy enough to purchase another one. For the child, however, this event can take on catastrophic proportions. Trying to reason a child out of his feelings about a dropped ice cream cone may be done with good intentions, but the difference in your mind-set is more likely to result in blocked communication than open communication.

Communication Blocks

The first step in creating an open line of communication with your child about school (or any other important subject, for that matter) lies in knowing what *not* to do. In his wonderful book, *Active Parenting*, Michael Popkin lists a variety of ways in which we speak to our children that invariably block, rather than open, communication.

Communication Block	How It Sounds
Commanding	*"Why don't you just stop worrying about school, you're only going to make it worse."*
Giving advice	*"Why don't you call some of your friends, then you'll feel better."*
Distracting	*"School, shmool, there's plenty of summer left. Why don't we take advantage of it and go to the movies?"*
Moralizing	*"Well, you know, school is good for you, and sometimes we have to do things we don't necessarily like to be better human beings."*
Sarcasm	*"For heaven's sake, nobody ever died from being nervous, you know."*
Being a know-it-all	*"School may seem tough now, but you'll be thankful one day that you went. Accumulating knowledge is the key to success in this world, take it from me. My grandfather didn't have the opportunities that you and I have, and I remember him saying to me . . . blah, blah, blah."*

Interrogating	*"What's wrong with school anyway? Did something happen there last year that you didn't tell me about?"*

During the many groups I lead, it's inevitable that when I speak about communication blocks, and give examples, there's a moment of silence when I finish. Then one parent will say "But if I can't use any of those, I won't be able to talk to my kids at all! What am I supposed to say?"

We're so used to using communication blocks that it does seem as if there are no other options when the blocks are taken away from us. Yet if you simply can refrain from responding with one of these blocks, you're already well on your way to opening up communication with your child. Even if you don't catch yourself using one of these, you often can tell if you've blocked communication by watching your child's face. If her eyes roll up in her head and the words "Oh, Mom (Dad), you just don't *get* it" come out of her mouth, chances are that you've blocked communication in some way. When we refrain from responding with a communication block, we free ourselves to actively hear our child's concerns, and we free our child to air her anxiety and thus alleviate it.

Actively Hearing Your Child

Being open to hearing what your child's concerns are means, first and foremost, being perceptive. Because elementary school children may still not be capable of telling you with words about their feelings, you must sharpen your powers of perception by using your eyes as well as your ears when trying to hear what your child has to say. Very often anxiety and stress are more likely to show on a child's face and in his body language than in the words he uses. When we watch our children for signs of stress (is she more irritable, does he cry more easily, is she withdrawn, does he "blow up" at the least little thing), our perceptiveness often can be the key to unlocking the stress.

"I noticed that Sam was having a great deal of difficulty staying in bed at night. Sometimes I'd hear him wandering around the house, and sometimes I'd get up in the morning and find him sleeping on the couch. He also started having accidents about once a week at night, which he hadn't had since he was toilet trained four years ago. I figured something must be up. So one day I sat him down and said, 'Sam, you seem a little disturbed about something, would you like to talk about it?' To my surprise, it was like I opened the floodgates. All this stuff about how difficult school was and how he wasn't sure he liked his teacher came pouring out."

Mom did a great job here! Her perceptiveness led her to comment about what Sam's feelings might be in this situation. While we can't always be sure about how our children are feeling, if we're hesitant in making a guess, as this mother was when she said "You seem a little disturbed about something, would you like to talk about it?" it often gives the child permission to talk about his anxiety. Just as children need a reflective mirror to help them see how they're dressed for the day, they need a reflective emotional mirror to help them see what's going on inside.

Feelings

Being perceptive about how your child is feeling, whether it is about school or anything else, is important to her emotional maturation. Part of our job as parents is to socialize our children. Socialization requires that they eventually learn how to see things from another person's point of view, to become sensitive to another person's feelings. In Dr. Ken Magid and Carole A. McKelvey's book *High Risk: Children Without a Conscience,* they say that children without consciences (child psychopaths) cannot feel remorse for even the most hideous crimes they have committed because they lack the ability to see other people as human beings with feelings and needs. This sensitization to feelings is important, and it begins with increasing a child's sensitivity to his own feelings.

Hundreds of Feelings

Most people are familiar with a small list of feeling words. If asked to name what feelings they most commonly have, they would probably say "angry, sad, happy, frustrated, and scared." Yet these are only five of the hundreds of feeling words we have in our vocabulary. Consider "overwhelmed," "disappointed," "energetic," "serious," "conniving," "insignificant." With each feeling word, a different "picture" of a person's emotional state comes to mind. Utilizing the wealth of feeling words at our disposal is important. If you simply label all of a child's negative feelings as "angry," you're liable to wind up with a child who acts in an angry way. But what if the child is really feeling discouraged? A discouraged child acts very differently from an angry child. Someone once told me that the Eskimos have more than a dozen words for snow. We might think that's going a bit overboard. Why would you need that many words for snow? Well, if you think about it, Eskimos live in a snowy environment, so it's necessary to their very survival to be able to differentiate between the types of snow. As human beings, we live in a *feeling* environment. It's just as necessary for us to be able to differentiate between the different types of feelings we have as it is for Eskimos to differentiate between the different types of snow. (Of course, Eskimos have it doubly hard, because they need to be able to differentiate between feelings too. They live in a snowy *and* a feeling environment.)

When you give children the vocabulary to tell the difference between the subtle shades of emotion they experience, you give them the opportunity to become aware of those same feelings in others and to become caring, conscientious, empathetic individuals.

Because many people don't necessarily have access to a list of hundreds of feeling words, I've included one here for your benefit.

Pleasant Feelings		Unpleasant Feelings	
accepted	high	afraid	jealous
adventurous	hopefil	angry	let-down
adequate	humble	anxious	lonely
amused	important	apathetic	miserable
bold	inspired	ashamed	nervous
brilliant	joyful	bashful	overwhelmed
calm	loving	bored	overworked
caring	lovely	cautious	pained
cheered	overjoyed	cheated	possessive
comfortable	peaceful	concerned	pressured
confident	peppy	confused	provoked
content	playful	cranky	pushed
creative	pleased	defeated	rejected
daring	proud	defiant	remorseful
delighted	refreshed	disappointed	resentful
eager	relieved	discouraged	shy
elated	satisfied	domineering	skeptical
encouraged	secure	down	stupid
energetic	snappy	embarrassed	suspicious
enthusiastic	sophisticated	envious	tired

excited	successful	foolish	threatened
fascinated	surprised	frustrated	trapped
free	sympathetic	guilty	uncomfortable
full	tender	hateful	uneasy
glad	tranquil	hesitant	unhappy
great	understood	hopeless	unloved
gutsy	warm	hurt	unsure
happy	wonderful	impatient	weary
helpful	zany	irritated	worried

How to Use Feeling Words

As your child begins to open up about school, *remember simply to listen.* When you do speak, restate what you hear, and watch for and reflect his emotions using one of the subtle feeling words from the list. Don't hesitate to use the more "advanced" words, even if you think they're not in your child's vocabulary. Often the word will resonate with your child's internal feeling and become connected, giving him access to it in the future. Talking about your child's feelings can alleviate much of his anxiety because it gives him permission to talk about them. You may not even have to do any more than just listen and reflect feelings; many times all your child needs to feel better is to feel heard and understood.

Listening is not always easy, however. What we often want to do as parents is insert our opinion, stories from our past, advice, or another of the communication blocks we've already talked about. Often keeping our mouths shut is the most difficult part of parenting. So, if you must speak, begin with the words "Seems like . . ." "Sounds like . . ." "I guess . . ." "What I'm hearing you say is . . ." With these beginnings it's difficult to block communication.

"My daughter came home from school the first two weeks saying she hated it. At first I kept trying to correct her, telling her that she didn't really 'hate' it, because 'hate' is such an unpleasant word. But things didn't get better. So I decided to try beginning with 'seems like . . .' and using a feeling word. The next time she complained, I simply said, 'It seems like you're having a tough beginning. You sound a little discouraged.' All she replied was 'Yeah,' so I thought maybe I'd lost her. I decided to keep at it though. I said, 'Sometimes it's uncomfortable when you go into a new class at the beginning of the year.' She replied, 'It is.' Still, I plugged away. I said, 'All those new faces, trying to get to know the new kids . . .' and I trailed off. Well, her face got this intense look on it 'Exactly!' she said. 'And there's this kid who keeps picking on me. I really hate him. I even cried yesterday.' Well, I was amazed! I had no idea she was being picked on in school."

Keep at It

Sometimes it's almost as if you have to drag information out of children. This mom did an effective job of "keeping at it" until she connected with her daughter, yet she wasn't pushy or forceful, nor did she block communication in any way. Her gentle reflective statements, made hesitantly through the use of phrases such as "seems like . . ." provided the support that her daughter needed to open up.

Each child is unique in his communicative ability or in his reticence to speak up. It seems as if some children are born communicators, talking about every feeling, thought, and event in their lives. For these children, even communication blocks may not deter them for long. Other children have difficulty expressing what goes on internally and even externally. For a child who has difficulty, it may take many attempts for you to open the lines of communication. Persistence, but not pushiness, is the key. For the resistant child, keep in mind these guidelines:

- Never try to force a child to talk.
- Take a casual approach. Rather than making a big deal out of sitting down for "a talk," initiate conversation when you're doing parallel activities—folding laundry, picking up at the end of the day, driving or walking to or from school.
- Try catching your child at her least resistant moment, perhaps in the few minutes right before she falls asleep.
- Look for openings that your child may present. "I hate school" or a mumbled "Everyone hates me" is a communication of feelings. Saying "sounds tough" in a sympathetic tone may get you further than you'd think.
- Avoid asking your child "why" she feels a certain way. Most of the time you'll just get a shrug and a mumbled "I don't know," and it usually serves to close down communication rather than opening it up. After all, if you have to ask "why," then you must not *really* understand how your child feels.
- If your child is extremely resistant, back off. Approach the subject in another way at another time. Very few things have to be handled as emergencies.

Matching Intensity

"When I try to talk to my son about feelings, it seems almost as if it irritates him more. I've used the 'seems like . . .' approach, and I think I've kept my tone of voice very sympathetic, but it's like it sends him off the deep end! He just gets more intense and seems angrier. The other day I met him after school and gave him a package of M&M's. In his haste to get the bag open, he ripped it quickly, spilling most of the bag onto the ground. He immediately got angry. When I said, 'Wow, seems like that made you feel angry,' he started to swing at me."

I've noticed that this reaction happens among a certain segment of the child population. I think it occurs because the child's intensity of feeling is vastly different from the parent's. So simply saying "seems like you feel angry" in a calm tone of voice doesn't begin to approach the intensity of the feeling that the child is experiencing. Thus the child still feels misunderstood. When children feel as if a parent doesn't understand them, they escalate their behavior in an effort to get you to understand. I have two suggestions that have helped the parents whose children react to sympathy in this way.

1. Instead of saying "seems like you're feeling angry" try saying "Gee, I really hate it when that happens."
2. Match the child's intensity to a certain degree. Try to imitate the tone of voice you hear him using.

"I tried that with my son the other day. We had a wonderful winter vacation together, but on the day he had to go back to school, he seemed really ferocious. He was slamming doors and screaming 'I hate school, I don't want to go back.' I began with saying sympathetically 'I guess it's hard to go back to school after such a nice vacation,' but that seemed to intensify his feelings. So I decided to refer to myself and match his intensity. In a frustrated and kind of angry tone of voice, I said, 'You know what? I hate going back after having such a nice time with you too. I am so frustrated that vacation isn't longer and that I have to go to my dumb old job again!' Well, do you know that he threw his arms around me?! It was like I'd finally 'gotten' what he'd been trying to say. We hugged for a while, and then we finished getting ready and he went to school without any other problems."

Keep in mind that children who respond to sympathy in this way are in the minority. As you begin identifying and reflecting your child's feelings about school and other subjects, start with the

simplest approach first, as suggested at the beginning
ter. Only if that approach seems to escalate the ch
feelings should you try being self-referential and usi
matches the intensity of the child's. In addition, tha..
child doesn't get the mistaken idea that your negative tone ot
voice is directed *at* him in some way but rather that it is a product of your ability to identify with his predicament.

Give a Measure of Control

The final step in setting your child up to succeed in school involves giving her some control over the routines and structure as-
sociated with school. Remember that going back to school is like
going back to work after a long and enjoyable vacation. Suddenly
you no longer designate what time to get up, what to wear, what
your schedule will be during the day, how you will spend your
time—these things are determined for you, by a preset schedule
to which you must adhere. For a child this lack of control can be
very anxiety provoking. By allowing your child to make some decisions about her time and how to use it, however, you give her
a reasonable amount of power, which will lessen her anxiety.

Using Choices to Give Control

We give our children a measured amount of control when we
employ structured choices. Children, like all human beings, have
needs that ultimately fulfill them as people. They need to be protected from physical and emotional harm; they need to have time
alone to think, feel, and become comfortable with themselves;
they need loving contact with other people; and they need to feel
appropriately powerful and in control of their own destinies. By
giving children choices, parents can give appropriate power to
their children. (We'll talk about how we can fulfill the other needs
our children have at other points in this book.)

What Kinds of Choices Are Helpful?

"What choice? As far as I can tell there are no choices. He has to be at school at a certain time, no ifs, ands, or buts. He has to do his homework, and he has to be in bed by a certain time. There is simply no room for argument."

It's true that your child has to do those things. But there are always choices within the choices. I'm not implying that he can choose not to go to school at all, or that he can choose what time to arrive. But if he has to be at school by 8:40, maybe he can choose whether to get up at 7:15 or 7:30. Maybe he needs a half hour after school to do homework, but perhaps he can choose whether to do it before or after dinner. Maybe he has to be in bed by 9:00, but perhaps he can choose how to organize the routine that precedes bedtime.

We do our children a great service when we recognize that within the boundaries that life (and likewise, school) imposes there are still choices available to us and to them. By offering these choices to our children, we give them enough power so that they feel in control.

Chapter 3
"I Hate Homework!"

Homework: The <u>Parental</u> Challenge

Many parents feel extremely challenged by their children's disinterest in and/or adamant refusal to do homework. Having been told by their children's teachers how vital a role they play in their children's success in school, they feel responsible for making their child attend to his homework. Using a variety of techniques, which usually include badgering, threatening, nagging, pleading, demanding, and yelling, among others, they succeed only in alienating their child and inadvertently pushing him further down the road of rebellion. But what's a parent to do? While we're told to be actively interested, we are not necessarily told how to communicate that interest. Instead of presenting ourselves as helpful, supportive, and understanding, we come across as dictators who have no real understanding of our children or their feelings. In other words, we put the homework above our children in importance. Our children wind up feeling misunderstood and even rebellious. So how do we put our children first yet still get the homework done?

The Homework Routine

We've said before that children thrive on routines. Homework is no exception. After-school time should be at least somewhat routinized (even if the routine must differ slightly from day to day because of after-school activities) so that the elementary school child has a sense of what your expectations are.

"But that's so hard! Every day is a little different, especially since I have two other children, one in junior high and one who's still a toddler. Most of the time we're trying to squeeze homework in somewhere between her dinner and my giving the baby a bath."

I know how hard it is to create a routine in the midst of what often appears to be chaos. But if you want your child to succeed in school, she must have both time and space set aside for her needs. If this means moving dinner a little earlier so that there's more time with Mom or Dad to help, or if it means dividing the homework up into several segments—some that she needs your help on, and some that she can do by herself—then do that. Each child is a little different, and it pays to understand what your child needs. Some children get along very well without parental supervision; others need the parent there the entire time. Remember that the effort you put into creating a routine will pay off well in the end as your child develops good study habits, a love for learning, and an understanding that education is important to her parents.

Work First, Play Later

"My child just procrastinates so much that it gets later and later until it's almost time for bed. First it's that she wants to practice her piano, which of course I want to encourage, then it's that she's hungry, couldn't she just have a snack, then her favorite program is on TV—the list is endless."

As I suggested when talking about the morning routine, sometimes we have to help our children adopt a "work first, play later" mind-set. Just like the morning routine, you want to build in motivation so that the child learns to work efficiently through her responsibilities in order to get to the things she wants to do.

"But my child really needs to run off some steam after sitting at school all day. If we come right home and do homework, it'll take twice as long because he'll be so wiggly in his seat."

Logistically speaking, it probably is better if homework follows playing outside or at a friend's house. Once you get home, however, homework should come *before* TV, dinner, telephone time, and so on. In this way, you can gently remind the procrastinating child that *"When* you've done your homework, *then* you can watch TV."

Corrections

"We have a pretty good routine, and I definitely have designated a space and a time for my daughter to do homework, but it's still like pulling teeth. She wiggles around, and we struggle back and forth over the interpretation about what the teacher wants in terms of answers. Then when I correct her if she gets something wrong, she blows up at me and it's another half hour before we can even get started again."

Unless you've been specifically requested to do so by your child's teacher, I suggest that you do not correct the homework. This may be a foreign concept to you, but it has many advantages. The first advantage is that your child's teacher then has the opportunity to truly evaluate your child's strengths and weaknesses based on her work at home. With this information, the teacher can more efficiently perform her job—to teach your child the things she doesn't yet understand. The second advantage is that by taking yourself out of the "correction mode," you can remain your child's advocate. This allows you to be a "cheerleader"—encouraging her, showing confidence in her ability, and generally supporting her as she goes about her responsibilities. It's difficult to say "I know it's hard. I'm sure you'll come up with the answer," then turn around and say "That's not the right answer!"

"My daughter came home from her first week of school with a lot more homework than she was used to. I could tell she was feeling overwhelmed and a little discouraged. She asked me to sit with her, and then spent the time dramatically draping herself in various positions all over the table and chair, complaining the whole time. I have to admit, I felt a little frustrated myself, and at first I kept saying things like 'Come on, just pick up the pencil and try. You haven't even looked at it.' But things just got worse. Then I remembered about reflecting her feelings, so I excused myself, got a drink of water, took a deep breath, and went back in. I said, 'I guess you're feeling a little discouraged.' 'It's too hard,' she whined. That kind of got my hackles up again, but I stuck in there. I said, 'Seems like it's a little overwhelming trying to get back in the swing of things.' Well, she responded positively to that, and so I kept reflecting her feelings, using words like 'frustrating,' and 'uncomfortable.' Finally I decided to see if there was a solution to this dilemma, and I said, 'Can you think of how you might feel less overwhelmed?' After a little hesitation, she asked if maybe she could take a break in between subjects. After that, things went along smoothly."

This dad did a terrific job! His responsiveness to his own building frustration led him to remove himself and think of a different way of handling the situation. Remembering about the importance of helping children feeling understood, he accurately identified and acknowledged his daughter's feelings. Then he took it one step further—he asked if there might be a solution to the problem. By asking his daughter if she could think of anything, rather than presenting a solution he might have thought of himself, he not only gave her the responsibility of solving the problem, but he empowered her in the process. But what if your child doesn't come up with a solution? What if she's so discouraged that she can't think of anything that would help? One mother handled it in the following way:

"I always make it a practice to sit with my daughter while doing her homework. One afternoon she began to whine 'I don't understand this, I can't do it.' I asked her what it was that she didn't understand, thinking I might be able to help her with it. 'I just don't know what I'm supposed to do.' I tried to explain the directions, but my daughter became more and more irritable, until she started shouting 'I just don't understand! I hate homework! I hate school.' Well, I began to feel completely exasperated with her. I tried to keep a clear head and think what Elizabeth might be feeling. Maybe she was frustrated, maybe overwhelmed, maybe nervous about getting the right answer. So I took a deep breath and said, 'I guess it feels pretty overwhelming,' at which Elizabeth burst into tears. So I went on and said, 'It can be pretty tough, especially when the directions don't seem clear.' Liz continued to cry and said, 'I just don't understand what the teacher wants.' So I said, 'Mm, yeah. I can tell you want to do the assignment well, and it's frustrating when you don't understand the directions and aren't sure exactly what the teacher is asking. I really would like to help, if I can. Is there anything I can do?' She continued to sob and was very negative. I decided to at least hesitantly offer some suggestions that I had thought of, so I said, 'You know, I can think of a couple of things, but I don't know if they'll help. Would you like to hear them?' To my surprise, she said she would. So I said, 'Well, one thing we could do is call one of your friends . . .' She definitely did *not* want to do that, so I just accepted that and went on. I said, 'Well, how about this? What about rewriting the directions to show the teacher what your interpretation is, then answer based on that? Then your teacher will know you tried, and if you're wrong, I'm sure she'll explain the directions and give you another chance.' But Liz didn't want to do that either. I tried a couple more times, but I felt myself getting frustrated with her negativity, so I finally told her that it was a hard problem and that I was going to take a break and think about it a little more. I suggested that maybe if she thought about it too, we might be able to come up with something."

The impressive thing in this story is that even though Mom was getting "shot down" at every suggestion, she didn't give in to her urge, which was to throw up her hands in disgust and walk away. What she did, however, was to suggest a short break to "think some more." Sometimes we wind up in a power struggle with our child, even if we utilize all the appropriate communication techniques at our disposal. When this happens it's like being in a sailboat during a hurricane. It's best to fold up the sail and sit tight, knowing that if the wind has nothing to blow against, the boat won't go anywhere. Mom did this when she suggested a little break. Mom continues the story . . .

"Well, I came back in a few minutes and I asked if she'd given it any more thought. She was still being very negative, and she said she just wanted to skip the whole thing. That she didn't want to do it at all. I guess at that point I figured I had nothing to lose, since it didn't seem we were getting anywhere anyway, so I asked her how she thought she'd feel if she went to school without her homework the next day. She really snapped at me and she said, 'I'd feel nervous. I hate school.' I don't know what made me stick with being sympathetic, but I guess I was in a 'zone.' So I said that I knew it was hard, and I understood how she felt. I remember saying 'Sometimes I guess you just feel so, I don't know, *stuck*, I guess. I wish I could help, I really do. I just don't know how. Do you have any suggestions as to how I can help?' And I don't know what happened, but it was like I'd broken through all of a sudden, and Liz sighed and said, 'Just stay here. I guess I'll do it the way I think it should be done and hope it's right.' "

This story really illustrates the benefits of "hanging in there" when your child is so discouraged that her negativity is getting in the way of problem solving or even in the way of your helping her. Mom's empathy and attempts to understand her daughter, which she successfully juxtaposed with open-ended questions to promote problem solving, worked to everyone's benefit in the end. Notice that when her daughter came up with the solution of not doing the homework at all, Mom didn't jump on this as an opportunity for argument or moralizing about handling responsibilities. Rather, she gave her daughter the opportunity to think through the potential consequence of not doing the homework at all.

So how do we do this in our own homes? First, know that when your child is having difficulty with homework, it's really up to him to come up with a satisfactory solution to the problem. This will help keep you from responding with one of the communication blocks we talked about in Chapter 2. Then follow this simple format:

1. Using the skills and feeling words you learned in Chapter 2, identify and reflect your child's feelings, saying "seems like . . ." "sounds like . . ." "I guess . . ." Do this a number of times, don't stop after just once. When a child is really feeling discouraged, he needs an opportunity to feel fully understood.

2. Support your child in coming up with a solution to the problem by saying "Can you think of anything you might do about this?" If you have suggestions, ask permission to state them, then phrase them in question form as in "What do you think would happen if you . . ." Graciously accept negative responses from your child.

3. Watch for your child's solutions, however inappropriate (as in "I just won't do it at all"). Help her think through the consequences of the solution she's proposing.

4. Finally, if your child is extremely negative, as Elizabeth was, take a break if you need to. Disengage gently, but firmly, and let the child know you'll be back.

When the Child's Procrastination Requires Discipline

"But what happens when being empathetic and engaging in problem solving isn't enough? There have been many evenings when my son and I are still doing homework at 11:30 at night."

Remember that the most important role you have as a parent is that of listener and empathizer. Many parents fear addressing their child's feelings about homework because they think it will make things worse or the job won't get done at all. But while the skills of listening and empathy may not seem to get you anywhere (or at least not quickly), they are often the fastest and most direct route to helping your child succeed.

Still, there are limits—both to your time and to your patience. I advocate that if you have a routine with built-in motivators, and you've been empathetic but there is still a problem, then it's time to enforce a few rules with specific consequences regarding homework.

1. Set a reasonable time limit during which your child must finish his homework.
2. Explain your expectations to your child and ask for his input.
3. Make any reasonable adjustments to the amount of time based on your child's input.
4. Explain to your child that you will make an attempt to help in whatever way possible, but if he exceeds the time limit because he's dawdling, unfocused, or misbehaving, then the homework will be put away for the evening. This will continue to happen each evening,

and if there is unfinished homework at the end of the week, he'll have to complete it all on Saturday morning prior to doing anything else.

Setting firm limits lets your child know you're serious about the value you place on homework. Explaining to him ahead of time how the consequences are going to work and that you're willing to help in whatever way possible helps him internalize the value behind the rule. In other words, the message to the child is "I value homework enough to help you with it and enough to make a rule about it as well."

Creating a Relationship with the Teacher

In order for this kind of rule to work with regard to homework, you probably will need to engage the help of the teacher. If you've been having difficulty with your child getting homework done, it's likely the teacher already knows about the problem (unless you've been successful, and the homework is complete each day). Schedule a conference with the teacher, letting her know that you're aware that there's a problem. In initiating a conversation rather than waiting for the teacher to come to you, you're more likely to gain the teacher's help. In the conference, reassure her that you value homework and that you're in the process of teaching your child this value. Explain that you've made a rule that will help you avoid unnecessary power struggles with your child. Tell your child's teacher that you are setting a limit on the amount of time you're allowing for homework in the evening, and that if your child procrastinates past the appointed time, you are going to have her finish the homework on Saturday. While this may mean a few weeks of homework coming in on Mondays, reassure the teacher that you think it will be a temporary situation and that if continues past two weeks, you'll meet with her again to discuss other alternatives.

The Parent-Teacher Relationship

Parents and teachers can work together or they can work against each other. When parents appear to be caring and concerned, and when they actively seek out the teacher in an attempt to work together, they usually find that the teacher will meet them halfway. If a teacher is not willing to meet concerned parents halfway, they may need to seek out the director or principal of the school.

"We had such a terrible experience with a teacher last year! Many of the instructions for the homework were completely open to interpretation, even from my point of view, but the teacher wouldn't take that into consideration when she was grading it. My daughter was consistently making poor grades, even though my wife and I could see nothing wrong with her answers. When we consulted the teacher we were basically told that we weren't being supportive and to keep out of it. We asked around and found out that a lot of other parents were having the same experience, and, in fact, only two children in the class were getting passing grades."

Speaking to the Principal or Director of Your Child's School

The first step in seeking the principal's help is to remember that you're not there to fight but rather to seek information or help that will be in the best interests of your child. Therefore, it is essential that you prepare ahead of time, so that you know what you're going to say and how you're going to say it. In order to advocate for your child in the best way possible, you'll want to keep the lines of communication open and be careful about your word choice so that the principal can hear what you have to say. Remember that it's likely the principal will have heard about the problem already from the teacher. In addition, he or she may feel the need to defend the teacher over your child.

Making Preparations

To prepare yourself to speak to the principal, write down all of the points you'd like to make. Don't concern yourself now with making them sound a certain way. If you feel defensive, write down defensive statements. Bob's list looked like this:

"I can't believe you hired that teacher in the first place, she's a moron!"

"You'd better do something about that teacher, or I'll see to it that your job is on the line."

"My kid is a bright child, and her grades better reflect that, or you're going to hear about it."

"I'll take this to the Board of Education if you don't cooperate."

As you can see, Bob feels angry and defensive. Writing his statements down on paper is a more productive way to vent his feelings rather than speaking them to the principal of his daughter's school. With a little help, he can make some of the same points in a more productive, communicative fashion.

Identifying Your Main Points

In looking over his list, Bob realized that some of his "statements" were empty threats, and some were simply name-calling. Neither of these is productive, particularly if you want to keep the lines of communication open! The real "points" Bob wanted to make were: "My child's grades aren't reflecting her intelligence," and "I'm seeking your help as the principal of the school about this issue."

Rephrasing Your Main Points

Now that Bob knows his main points, he must phrase them in a way that will not raise defenses. I asked him to see if he could either phrase his statements as questions or include feelings. Here is what he came up with:

"I feel confused about my daughter's grades. How can I best work with the school to help her grades reflect her intelligence?"

If you use feeling words such as "confused," "helpless," "concerned," "bewildered," you normally will elicit an empathetic helping response from the listener. Consider the difference between Bob's rephrasing and what he could have said: "I feel angry about my daughter's grades," or "I feel frustrated about my daughter's grades." Both of these statements are more likely to raise the principal's defenses. Bob reported that his conversation with the principal went something like this:

Bob began by saying "I'm here because I'm feeling concerned and a little confused about my daughter's grades. I thought that maybe if I spoke with you about it, you could give me an idea of how I can work with the school and with her teacher in the most productive way." "Have you spoken with the teacher?" "Yes," replied Bob, "I did, briefly. I seem to have gotten off on the wrong foot with her, though, and I'm just not sure how to work it out. I really want to be supportive of the school and help my daughter at the same time."

Bob did a great job here. Rather than saying he'd spoken to the teacher and she was unreasonable, or uncommunicative, he put it back on himself, which did him no harm, and probably helped his daughter's case. The principal replied:

"Well, what seems to be the problem?" Bob then produced some of the homework sheets and said, "Well, I think the issue is the way my daughter interprets the homework. You can see that on these sheets, if you take her interpretation, the answers are right. I guess my question is how can I help her interpret the instructions in the same way that the teacher does?" The principal looked for a long time at the sheets, and Bob remained silent. "Hmm," she said. "Well, Mr. Hanson, I appreciate your coming in. Let me speak to the teacher and I'll get back to you."

Bob and I had talked about the fact that it was unlikely the principal would side against the teacher in his presence. So in spite of this semiabrupt ending, which seems to have no real conclusion, Bob had a feeling that he'd made his point. He thanked the principal and said he would look forward to hearing what she thought about how he could help. Interestingly, the principal did not follow up, but the instructions on the homework sheets changed significantly within a week, and Bob's daughter, as well as others in the class, began getting better grades.

When the Principal Doesn't Respond Well

But what if the principal still doesn't respond well? What if she'd said, "Look, Mr. Hanson, your daughter is going to just have to learn to deal with this," and sent him packing?

Chances are that most principals won't respond this way. But if this is the case, the you'll need to weigh your options. Is it worth spearheading a concerned parent group and taking the matter up with the principal in force? Or is it worth going over the principal's head? If that should work, the payoff is clear. What if it doesn't work, however? What would the consequences be to your child if your best efforts fail and she has to remain in the class? Each situation is different, and it's important to think through both the payoffs and the consequences for your actions. Meanwhile, regardless of what you choose, you can still empower your child to handle the situation in the best possible way.

Empowering Your Child

What is empowerment? Empowerment means "to enable," "to give power to," "to provide with the means or the opportunity." Difficult situations are an opportunity for us to teach our children how to handle life. All of us, at one point or another in our lives, have encountered difficult people or situations, strife, or unpleasantness. Many times we even had to live with an unpleasant situation for a period of time. Successful people are those who figure out how to cope within these situations, not necessarily get out of them.

When we allow our children to vent their feelings, when we admit that our feelings are similar, and when we brainstorm with our children about how to make the best of a bad situation, we give them the resources that will allow them to help themselves through life's difficulties in the future. If Bob's situation hadn't turned out so well, he could have told his daughter that he'd tried to rectify it but that it seemed as if it was going to continue to be unfair. He then could have listened to his daughter's feelings about the unfairness of the situation and agreed about how hard that was. (But *not* said, "Life is unfair sometimes, we have to learn to live with it," which would block communication!) Then he could have asked if she'd like his help brainstorming to see if there was a way to work around the situation or a way to learn to live with it. Maybe they would have decided together that as unfair and unreasonable as it felt, presenting the teacher with two different versions of the homework would help. Or maybe they would have decided that they would examine past homework assignments to see if they could get a handle on a common interpretation that the teacher was using. Maybe they could contact the few students who were getting better grades and ask for help interpreting the homework. Whether Bob's daughter accepts one of these solutions or not, all of them will help her realize that even within a bad situation, there are alternatives. With this realization, she can feel capable and confident in her ability to cope with life's difficulties, and she need never feel "stuck" or helpless, as so many of us do when strife rears its ugly head.

Chapter 4

Extracurricular Overload

Today there are more choices for our children's extracurricular lessons than ever before. Should we enroll our children in music school, art classes, theater programs? Wouldn't karate help them learn self-defense? What about having them audition to be in professional ballet programs, or would it be better to give them a more diverse dance background? And don't forget about sports! We've heard that when boys or girls are part of a team, they learn cooperation and teamwork. So maybe we should also pursue soccer, Little League, basketball. Then there are piano lessons. After all, shouldn't everyone know how to play the piano? Don't forget swimming . . . every child needs to learn how to swim, if only for safety's sake during summer vacations! The list is endless. The wealth of choices, combined with working parents' need to have their children supervised until after work hours and the financial constraints that each individual family faces, can make it difficult to decide what, as well as how many of the various activities, classes and experiences are appropriate for our children.

Most parents want the best for their children, so with the best of intentions, they sign their children up for a full load of extracurricular activities. But when does a good thing turn into too much of a good thing? How much is too much for an elementary school child?

No Easy Answers

The answer is not an easy one, because every child is different. An extracurricular load that might be just right for one child might be disastrous for another. Your child's age, temperament, interests, and activity level as well as your needs and financial constraints must be considered when choosing appropriate classes or activities. Keep in mind, however, that no matter what your child's age, *any* child can fall victim to extracurricular overload. In your zest to expose your children to the opportunities, don't fail to recognize the warning signs of burnout. Catching this early can help prevent it from worsening and resulting in an unhappy, stressed, fatigued child whose schoolwork, social life, and home life suffer.

The Warning Signs of Burnout

To determine if your child has fallen victim to extracurricular overload, ask yourself the following questions:

- Does your child seem fatigued, irritable, or lacking in energy on a particular day of the week?
- Does your child complain about headaches, stomachaches, sore throat, or other physical ailments regularly? Is there a pattern to his complaints? Does the pediatrician say there's nothing physically wrong?
- Does your child cry easily, become moody or withdraw when she's not being actively distracted?
- Is your child unusually aggressive on a particular day of the week?
- Has your child ever mentioned not wanting to be involved in a particular activity for which he's signed up?

If you answered "yes" to any or all of these, especially if a pattern of behavior has emerged (i.e., your child only complains about going to school or feeling ill on a particular day of the week when an extracurricular activity is scheduled), then it's possible he or she is experiencing extracurricular overload. The first step in treating this ailment lies in encouraging an open discussion with your child.

Facilitating an Open Discussion

The most important thing you can do when you sit down to discuss extracurricular activities with your child is to adopt a nonjudgmental attitude. If your child feels as if you'll be angry that she doesn't want to play basketball or take swimming, she's not likely to be honest with you.

"You know, when I first signed my son up for karate we were both enthusiastic. I really thought it would help him learn discipline and coordination as well as self-defense. He liked the idea of being in the same class as his buddies. By the middle of the second semester, though, I realized that it was a struggle to get him to pack his uniform and that he was always saying he was tired or sick on the day he had karate. When I finally asked him whether he wanted to continue or not, he said he did, but he had a funny look on his face—kind of guilty or something. When I pressed a little more, and I actually told him, 'You know, I won't be mad if you don't want to go,' he got this look of relief, like he'd been carrying a weight around, and he said, 'Really? I thought you'd be really mad!' It was then that I realized how much of what *I* wanted had gone into this. Thinking back even further, I saw that he had probably been picking up on my tone of voice and maybe feeling pressured all along."

Many children hide their true feelings in an effort to please their parents. Some children just may not be cut out to be a black belt in karate, a prima ballerina, or a soccer player, but because they sense that Mom or Dad wants them to do this, they won't speak up on their own behalf. This hesitancy contributes to the stress they may already be feeling from having too many scheduled activities each week. In order to facilitate communication, it may be necessary to examine your own feelings or attitude about the particular activities you've signed your child up for, and I would encourage you to do this *before* you actually sign him up. Think back . . . Did you always consider yourself a klutz but secretly long to be on the basketball or football team? Were you an adequate musician but aspired to greatness? Do you regret that you never stuck with your training for and/or dream to be in the Olympics? Is it even remotely possible that you'd like for your child to be what you never could be, for whatever reason?

It's not uncommon for parents to pass on their wishes, their desires, their hopes and dreams to their children. Often, however, this doesn't produce Olympic gymnasts but unhappy children instead. When you sit down with your child to develop an extracurricular plan or to evaluate the one you already have, feel free to say to that you want your child to be happy in the activities you choose together. If you know that being a concert pianist was your unfulfilled heart's desire, admit it to her, and let her know that just because it was something you wanted, you don't expect her to want it as well. Encourage her honesty, and tell her that no matter what she chooses to do after school, you love her just because of who she is, not because of what she chooses to study.

When Your Child Wants to Do Too Much

"But what happens when the shoe is on the other foot? When it's our *children* who want to do more, or do things we think are unrealistic? What happens if we feel that they're doing too much already? My son seems to be interested in everything. And in all honesty, he's also very talented at many things. But first of all, we can't afford everything, and second, I'd rather have him concentrate on a few activities and do them well than do a lot of activities and be only average."

If your child seems to be talented and enthusiastic in a lot of different activities, then elementary school is the ideal time to let him try as many as possible, as long as you can afford it and as long as he doesn't experience burnout. Only by trying will he eventually weed out the things he doesn't want to do and ultimately concentrate on those things he does want. To expect your child to "master" even a few activities at this developmental stage is a bit unrealistic. The elementary school child really should be a "jack of all trades" if he's capable. With age and development, he'll begin to make decisions about what his passions are and drop the things that don't interest him.

If, however, you're afraid your child will let her schoolwork suffer, or if you can't afford to pay for all the extracurricular activities she wants to be involved in, then the communication skills you've been learning in this book will be useful.

The first thing to do is set time aside to speak to her about her schedule rather than making decisions "on the fly." Often children will enthusiastically bring up a new class they've heard about when it pops into their heads, which is not necessarily the best time to have a discussion. Rather than reacting, tell your child that it sounds interesting and that you'll put it on the agenda for a family meeting.

Family Meeting?

Family meetings are a useful tool for many families. Basically, all a family meeting requires is that you set aside time on a regular basis to discuss matters of importance to the whole family.

"You've got to be kidding! Have a 'family meeting'? That's just too rigid! My kids will never go for it, and besides, it sounds more like something you'd do in business, not in a family. I want my family to have a 'family feel.' "

In every group and workshop I teach, there are always some people who resist the idea of family meetings. I'll never forget a beginning workshop I taught a number of years ago where a husband and wife attended, both of whom were lawyers. Highly intelligent people, who also cared deeply about doing the right thing for their son, then maybe three years old, they enthusiastically absorbed every particle of information I doled out. Until we got to family meetings. Then two sets of eyeballs began to roll, and I could tell that they were resistant. I encouraged them to use the other techniques and if they felt uncomfortable with the idea of family meetings, to just keep it on the "back burner." As loving parents, they continued after the beginning workshop, devoting part of their busy and precious time to come to an advanced course I give. One big issue they were having with their son at the time was persuading him to allow them to wash his hair. They'd tried almost every technique in the book, and nothing seemed to work. Finally, at one session, they came in and said their son finally was allowing his hair to be washed, if not with enthusiasm, at least without a struggle. Astonished, the group asked how they did it! Both looked sheepish, and admitted "we had a family meeting."

The Benefits of Family Meetings

As rigid as it may sound, this technique works! And the truth is that children actually like family meetings. My own children often call a spontaneous family meeting because they have something they want to discuss that "won't wait" until the next scheduled time.

The benefits of having meetings as a family are far reaching. First, and perhaps most important, family meetings give children a sense that they are part of something bigger than themselves and help them recognize their interdependence. They learn that they are important cogs in a wheel and that without their coop-eration, the family simply wouldn't work as well. In addition, when children are included in the decision making and problem solving that occurs during these meetings, they learn how deci-sions are made and problems are solved—both important life skills. Children also learn about compromise, because the deci-sions you make as a family may not always be what each indi-vidual wants but rather those that each individual can, at least, live with.

Essentially, family meetings give the message that being a member in a family is important. That each individual in a family is a human being with needs and wishes. That the family con-siders each person important enough to listen to. Whether your family consists of two people or ten, these meetings will help give it substance and strength.

What's in a Family Meeting?

More than anything else, a family meeting is simply scheduled time. Most families find it helpful to have their meetings on week-ends, usually at the beginning of the day, before everyone scatters according to their own agendas. Having a meeting on a weekend also helps you discuss how the weekend will proceed and what's coming up during the next week that might impact the whole family. It's helpful to post an "agenda" of sorts somewhere ac-cessible to all family members. That way those who already know how to write can mark down items they'd like to bring up. Kinder-garten and first graders just learning to write will, of course, have to ask for help in writing down items of importance to them.

How to Start Your Meeting

How you proceed with your meeting is really up to you. Re-member, though, that elementary school children like, and can re-late to, a certain level of formality and structure. Many schools have "meeting time" as part of the school day, so the concept may not be entirely unfamiliar to your child. Let's see how the family with the hair-washing problem runs their meetings:

"Well, the first thing we do is talk about what went *right* over the past week. That way, we set the tone of the meeting as positive. We also remember to thank each other for any help a family member might have given to another member during the past week. For example, my husband thanked my oldest son (who's now eight, by the way) for mopping up some water that had spilled in the bathroom. Then we look at the agenda, which we keep posted on the refrigerator, and read the items. We try to have our family meetings last only about thirty minutes, so we order the items in importance, keeping in mind that each member of the family needs to have at least one of their agenda items heard. Then we just go down the items one by one, and if we don't get to them all in the allotted time, we schedule a short, less formal meeting for another time, usually the next day. We've also found it helpful to write down important decisions that we make during a meeting, because we discovered that if a decision isn't entirely to another member's liking but wasn't written down, it can be cause for debate and argument when we're trying to enforce it later."

Discussing Extracurricular Activities at a Meeting

"We decided that before signing Sarah up for a lot of after-school things, we'd bring it up at a family meeting. We started out by telling her that it was going to be our primary topic, and we were interested in her ideas, interests, and opinions. We said that the final decision would be agreed upon by all of us and that we had to have some say because we simply couldn't afford to do absolutely everything. We agreed that we wouldn't discuss finances, though, until we'd brainstormed about everything she was interested in."

Brainstorming is a wonderful way to get the most out of a family meeting on any topic. When brainstorming, the idea is to come up with as many alternatives as possible, without editing for any reason until you have as long a list as possible. While some of the alternatives or ideas may seem silly, inappropriate, or unfeasible, if you refrain from criticizing them, it's possible that ultimately one might lead to the ideal solution or alternative.

"We used brainstorming when talking about Josh's after-school schedule. It worked surprisingly well. One of the things he said he was interested in was deep sea diving—how unrealistic can you get? But because we were brainstorming, we let it ride. The surprising thing was, though, that it led his sister to say 'How about snorkeling?' We wrote that down too. Then my husband said, well, how about taking swim lessons now, and this summer, maybe we can vacation at a spot where you can learn snorkeling or deep sea diving? So now Josh is happily enrolled in swim lessons, which isn't something we necessarily would have thought of before!"

Being Clear About Expectations

After you've laid out all the possibilities, and before you make a final decision, it's important to be clear with your child about what your expectations might be—not only with extracurricular activities, but with schoolwork and chores as well. For example, do some of the possibilities you've listed require practice time? Will you expect that your son spend a certain amount of time practicing? When does he think he'll fit that in? In addition, will you be committing to a semester of lessons? A full year? What if he tires of them halfway through? Are your expectations that he must complete the commitment? Or would you allow him to drop out if he found the activity wasn't to his liking after all? In addition, your child should know that you will still expect him to get his homework done nightly by a certain time and to do his chores routinely. Now is also a good time to spell out what will happen if his grades start to slip or chores aren't completed on time. Maybe you'll decide that his extracurricular activities will be curtailed for a specific length of time if this happens, or that the chores will all have to be done on the weekend. Many parents find it helpful to put this "agreement" in writing, having both parent and child sign it so that there's no "confusion" in the future about what the details of your agreement were.

"That makes it sound so serious and discouraging, though. If I were a kid, I wouldn't want to sign up for something that had all those warnings attached!"

It is important not to come across too negatively. I remember quite recently, as a matter of fact, when I was taking my daughter to school and I heard a mother talking to her son about his desire to take cello lessons. She was saying "But that's such hard work, and it's such a difficult instrument to play. Do you know how awful it sounds when you don't really know how, and you make all those mistakes? And the cello is so heavy! How do you think you'll even get it around? Why don't you take something easier, like guitar? Guitars aren't nearly as difficult . . ." As she talked, I could see her son getting more and more discouraged until he finally said, "Nah, I don't want to take guitar. I guess I'll just stick with soccer."

The best way to ensure that your child doesn't feel overwhelmed with negativity as the child in the last scenario did is to begin by being enthusiastic about her choices. By saying something like "Wow, these are great choices, and I know you'll do well with all of them," or "These sound like really fun activities to try," you can set your child up to succeed rather than have her give up before even trying. After you've made a positive comment, then you could simply say "Now let's talk about the best way to organize things so you can get in the practice time (or homework or chore time) you'll need."

Finishing Commitments

"What happens if you sign your kid up for two or three activities because you think he can handle it only to find out in the middle of the semester that it really is too much? We did that last year, and we really thought he could handle three days of sports, because he's so active. But halfway through, it was apparent that he was suffering from burnout. I couldn't get my money back, though, and I also felt it was important to carry through on the commitment he'd made, so I made him complete the semester. Was that wrong?"

If it becomes apparent in the middle of a semester that you've made a mistake, either because it's "too much" or because it's clear that your child is bored or dislikes a particular activity, you certainly do not have to pull him out immediately and lose your tuition. While we must recognize and respect our children's needs, we also must balance our decisions with common sense. If it's going to cost you hundreds of dollars to pull out of an activity in the middle, then explain to your child why you're requesting that he finish his commitment. Finishing out a few weeks or even a month or two of a particular activity is not likely to damage your child permanently. Just consider it a lesson learned, have him finish the session, and do things differently the next time.

Chapter 5
"Can I Have a Play Date?"

Just as part of our job as parents is to encourage and support our children in their academic growth, so too must we support the development of their social skills. Nowhere can this development take place more readily than when our children are encouraged to play with their peers or to sleep over at another child's house.

The Value of Play

Play is an essential part of your child's world. When a child plays, she has the opportunity to put herself in someone else's shoes for a little while. How does that feel? When your son "becomes" Superman, he experiences what it's like to act heroically. When your daughter "becomes" a doctor, she understands the seriousness of someone else's illness and what it feels like to help heal that person. In playing "Mommy" and "Daddy," your children experiment with nurturing their doll "baby." Playing helps your child learn about himself and about his environment—just as baby animals play at catching prey before they're actually required to do so for survival purposes.

Likewise, children can try out different ways of responding or interacting with others under the guise of "pretend." Sometimes they are even working out things that actually happened to them. Perhaps a friend was nasty to your son at school. Later, at home with another friend, you might hear your son responding to him in a rude way. In all likelihood, he's discovering how it feels to be on the "giving" end of the rudeness. Because he feels safe with his peer, he knows that his rudeness won't destroy the underlying relationship, which allows him to experiment a little.

In play, our children manipulate objects, count, develop their fine and gross motor coordination, learn about physics and science. And the learning doesn't stop indoors. The playground is another place where social and physical challenges are met, dealt with, and overcome. It is an arena where our children can thrive in the format where they function best—play. And it is, therefore, an important and basic component of their developing self-esteem. Quite simply, the stakes aren't high in the arena of play whereas they might be very high in the "real" world. With lower stakes, our children feel freer to discover who they are and who they might become.

When playing indoors or out, at your home or in the home of a friend, your children have the opportunity to stretch and challenge themselves emotionally in safe surroundings. And in stretching their imaginations just a little beyond their current capabilities, they grow socially.

Facilitating the Play Experience

In order for our children to get the most out of their play experience, it is important that we, as adults, do not succumb to our need for control at the expense of our children. Very often we step into children's play when stepping in is unnecessary.

"My child is so rude and bossy. When I hear her playing with certain of her friends, I just get nuts. Everything always has to be her way."

While parents who hear their children behaving this way with friends can become very concerned, exerting control in this situation doesn't allow our children to achieve the growth potential that playing with peers can accomplish. In addition, many times the children actually switch "bossy" roles—but because you're only the parent of one of the children, you have a tendency to hear only your own child being bossy. Allowing your child to self-regulate her behavior with her peers ultimately will result in a more equal peer relationship with her friends.

"But what happens when we have to step in? I mean, let's say we hear our kid fighting with her friend. As parents, don't we have to step in and control that?"

Not necessarily. I think one thing that "fools" parents into involving themselves is the intensity with which children converse, fight, and, yes, play. An exchange of similar intensity between adults would be taken very seriously. But it's important to keep in mind that the same intensity in children doesn't necessarily mean that someone is going to get hurt.

"The other day, my daughter and her friend were in the bedroom. All of a sudden, I heard an argument break out that sounded terrible. But I decided to wait and see what happened instead of running into the room. I listened a bit longer and even got close to the door where they couldn't see me. As I listened, I realized that they were role-playing—my daughter was pretending to be someone named Samantha, and her friend was 'being' Jane. The fight I'd heard was part of their play!"

A disadvantage of stepping in when our children are playing with their peers is that very often we step in on behalf of the other child, even when we have no idea what is happening. This sends a loud and clear message to our own child that we are not his or her ally. More than almost anything else, our children need for us to be on their side. They rely heavily on us for support and guidance, but if we consistently take another's side over theirs, they soon learn that we can't be trusted to support them. That trust in our support is crucial if we ultimately are to be able to instill our values in our children. Now, that's not to say that if your child just clobbered another kid over the head with a baseball bat, you should take your child's side! Clearly, discipline is called for when someone gets hurt. In general, however, I would urge you to adopt a wait-and-see policy before stepping into your child's play or conflicts with a friend.

The Benefits of "Wait and See"

This wait-and-see attitude can be beneficial to your children in many ways. By refraining from intervening too quickly, you might discover, and help your children discover, that they can be very adept at solving their own conflicts. In this discovery, they develop social confidence, which helps build their self-esteem. In addition, the more confidence they have solving their own problems, the less likely they are to run to an adult for help each time something comes up. This movement toward independent problem solving lays a good groundwork for the preteen and teen years when children need good conflict resolution and problem-solving skills.

"I took a wait-and-see attitude with my son and his friend. They were definitely having a real conflict, but it was clear that they weren't going to come to physical blows, so I just listened. They were very rude to each other for a little while, and the insults really flew. Then there were a few minutes of silence. Maybe they were both pouting, I'm not sure. I was surprised when I heard my son propose a solution. At first, his friend wouldn't take him up on it, but my son did a bit of negotiating and *voilà!* The conflict was resolved!"

Why We Intervene

This father did a good job; for most parents, it seems to be very difficult not to jump in. One of the reasons for this is that we have a strong moral opinion that we wish to get across to children. "Fighting isn't nice," "It's rude to act like that with a friend," "It isn't polite to always demand your way" are thoughts that occur to many parents when they hear children fighting. This is further complicated when other parents or people are present. When we're in our homes, our thoughts often go something like this: "Oh, my God, _____ must think I'm a terrible parent for not reprimanding my child!" On the playground, our thoughts run more along the lines of "Everyone is looking at me." When we're embarrassed or uncomfortable, we have a tendency either to come down harder on our children than we normally would or to undermine them in front of others in order to "save face" or "explain" their (or our own) behavior. Yet when we do this, we sacrifice our children's self-esteem and rob them of the opportunity to take full advantage of the social enrichment that playing and even conflicting with a friend can produce. In addition, most of the time our intervention isn't even very effective.

"My daughter and her friend were sitting at the table, and I was cooking dinner. They were drawing, and I heard my daughter making comments like 'That's an ugly drawing you're making.' Well, I tried not to intervene, but I just couldn't help myself. I told her that it wasn't very nice to talk that way. She turned to me and said, 'Well, she's stupid!' Meanwhile, her friend seemed totally unaffected by all of this. So my daughter and I continued to argue for a little bit, and then I finally gave up and went back into the kitchen. I heard her make a few more rude remarks to her friend, then her friend said something that I didn't hear, and within five minutes they were best buddies again."

When You Must Intervene

"But aren't there times when we have to intervene? My son is very physical, and I'm afraid that when he gets really mad, he and his friends will come to blows."

It's clear that there are times when we, as parents, must step in. Let's take a look at a model for conflict resolution that encourages independent problem solving and helps build children's confidence and self-esteem.

A Model for Helping Children Resolve Conflict

The first step in resolving children's conflict is to stop, look, and listen. This is the wait-and-see philosophy I've already talked about. To determine whether the children really need your intervention, ask yourself these two questions:

1. Is someone being physically or emotionally hurt?
2. Has a child come to you for help?

If you answer "yes" to either of these, then the children need your help and you need to intervene.

Establishing Emotional Hurt

"My daughter has never been physically aggressive, so none of her conflicts would ever involve physical harm. But she has a sharp tongue, and I know that sometimes it hurts her friend's feelings. Should I step in when children's feelings are being hurt?"

This is a tricky question, because while there's often no doubt as to what physical harm looks like, emotional damage can be much more difficult to establish. To determine whether a child is being emotionally hurt (as opposed to having temporarily hurt feelings), you'll need to take into account a number of factors: the specific words, tone of voice, gestures, and facial expressions you see or hear; the personality of the child whom you think is being emotionally hurt; and the history of the relationship between the children.

Words, Tone of Voice, Gestures, and Facial Expressions

One way to determine whether emotional damage is taking place is to pay close attention to the words and tone of voice you hear used, combined with the response they elicit from the child who is the recipient. Watching the recipient's facial expression and body language *over a period of time* can provide clues as to whether emotional damage is taking place. If one child says, "You're a dork brain," and the other child rolls his eyes and goes about his business, for example, you can be relatively sure that this is not emotionally hurtful. On the other hand, if one child says nastily, "I'm never going to be your friend again, and I'm telling everyone at school that you still sleep with your teddy bear," and the other child responds by pleading "I'm sorry, please. I'll do anything you want. Please don't tell anyone. You'll stay my friend, okay?" then I would be concerned.

Personality

A child's personality also must be considered when determining whether you think he's being permanently hurt by another child's words. For example, if a child is highly emotional and tends to cry easily, then when he cries, it may *not* be an indication that any deep emotional damage is being inflicted. If, however, a child is normally stoic, and you see her responding to another child's comments by holding back her tears, it may be a sign that adult intervention is necessary.

History of the Relationship

If your child has an unbalanced relationship with a friend where one party is consistently the victim, or underdog, or where one of the children appears to be getting more and more discouraged by the exchanges that take place, this too might indicate that an adult's intervention is necessary. If, over time, however, it appears that the relationship is relatively equal, with one child being "bossy" some of the time and the other child dictating the activities and rules at other times, then there's probably no need to worry when bossiness or rudeness occasionally occurs.

Discard Your Peacemaker Role

"When my daughter's best friend comes over, which is often, the level of chaos in my house seems to increase a hundredfold. So when they fight, they may not be physically or emotionally hurting each other, but all I can think is that I just want to keep the peace."

One of the most difficult parts of this model is that parents have to get rid of their peacemaker role. We tend to put up with the chaos, though it wears on our patience, until a conflict occurs. Then, because we're already stretched thin and all we can think of is having a little peace and quiet, we barge in and take over. This may resolve the conflict temporarily, but it doesn't allow the play process to enrich our children's social development. Rather than jumping in at the point of conflict, I urge parents to set up some house rules to bring the chaos down to a dull roar. Later in this chapter we'll discuss how to go about setting up and enforcing house rules. Meanwhile, once the children are in conflict, it's important to remember that keeping the peace is not our main objective.

Focus on Feelings

Once you've decided that intervention is necessary, the first thing to do is to focus on the children's feelings. In doing so, you will increase their awareness of and sensitivity to each other's feelings. This is a crucial ingredient in helping a child evolve into an empathetic, caring, and moral adult. Before a child can be aware of someone else's feelings, however, he must be aware of and comfortable with his own feelings.

In focusing on feelings, we also convey the underlying message: "You are important to me. I want to understand why you feel the way you do." This maintains the integrity of our relationship with our own child and ultimately makes him more open to hearing the values we so desperately want to impart.

When children are in conflict, you must reflect both children's feelings back to them. Doing so will not only help both children feel understood (which is sometimes enough to diminish the fighting), it will help them learn to communicate their feelings with words rather than fists, yelling, or sulking.

"My son, Matthew, and his friend Jordon were fighting about who was going to get to use the computer first, and I was concerned that someone was going to get hurt, because they were getting rough. I chose to intervene and remembered about focusing on feelings. So I said, 'Wow, seems like you guys are having a problem.' They started with the old 'Well, he did this . . .' and 'Did not, he started it . . .' I said, 'Matt, you seem angry with Jordon, and I hear that Jordon, maybe you're feeling defensive.' They looked a little stunned but continued with their blame strategies, so I hung in there and said, 'Sounds like sometimes it's a little frustrating trying to work things out.' At that point, I guess they realized that I wasn't going to take sides, so they both just muttered, 'Yeah,' and scowled at each other."

Dad did a great job practicing late intervention here. When he realized that someone might get hurt, he stepped in and remained focused on the kids' feelings. You can see from the dialogue that when Dad stepped in, the children automatically assumed that he was going to play "judge and jury," so they turned their attention away from resolving their conflict and onto "making a case" for themselves. Had Dad actually handed down a verdict, the final lesson would have been about winning rather than negotiating, communicating, and ultimately problem solving. Let's see what Dad did next.

Helping the Children Brainstorm

"Once the kids were just glaring at each other, I recognized that they probably at least felt that their feelings had been heard, if not by each other, at least by me. So I said, 'Can you guys think of any way you might be able to work this out?' Of course, they immediately started up again: 'No way, I'm not cooperating with him,' and 'There's no way to work it out.' I stayed calm and commented, 'Yeah, I guess it feels that way sometimes,' then I said, 'Hmmm. I wonder what would happen if you guys played separately for a while?' Well, immediately I got 'No way!' which when you think about it is kind of funny since they weren't playing well together in the first place. So then I said, 'I wonder what would happen if you guys just put the computer away altogether and played something else?' This time they were less vociferous, but I still got a mumbled 'no.' So then I said, 'This is a sticky problem. Sometimes it's difficult to come up with a solution. You guys have a great way of working things out though, and I know you'll come up with something. I'll be really interested in what you decide to do.' "

In working through some possibilities with the children, Dad not only diminished their anger further but began the process of teaching good problem-solving skills. He remembered to begin with "Can you think of anything . . ." which sent the message to the children that the responsibility for coming up with a solution was really in their hands. Even though they responded negatively, Dad didn't get discouraged and become negative himself. He continued with a couple of his own suggestions, carefully beginning with "I wonder what would happen if . . ." to frame his ideas as questions. Once he saw that the anger had diminished sufficiently, he made a closing comment that was encouraging in nature, saying essentially that he knew how tough it was and that he felt confident in the children's ability to work things through.

In taking the time to help the children with their feelings and to brainstorm solutions with them, Dad did a number of things that will have far-reaching effects. He helped each child become more aware of his own feelings, with the knowledge that that awareness eventually will help them both learn to express their feelings with words, not with fists or loud abusive language. By recognizing *both* children's feelings, he showed that others have feelings too. In framing his comments as questions and in ultimately leaving the solution up to the children, he encouraged cooperation and negotiation, and moved these children down the path toward becoming independent problem solvers.

Establishing House Rules

"I don't really have a problem with conflict between my son and his friend. But I do have a problem with the mess. One kid in particular has absolutely no respect for the 'house rules' when he comes over to play. After every play date, the place is a wreck, with toys all over the place. He never picks up after himself, and my son ends up completely overwhelmed with the clean-up afterward."

When our children choose friends who behave in ways that violate our values, it can create some tough choices for us as parents.

I'm not talking about shockingly inappropriate behavior. Obviously, if the behavior is extreme, you'll have to insist that your child not see that friend. But most children's behavior isn't so outrageous that parents would be willing to "ban" a friend completely from the house. At the same time, it seems difficult for many parents to enforce the rules that communicate our values with other people's children.

Truthfully, enforcing the "house rules" that communicate your values should not be so different with your child's friends from with your own child. The key in both cases is to communicate your expectations respectfully, honestly, and clearly, and to set up ahead of time some well-defined consequences for rules that get broken.

Respect

Many times parents feel doubtful about establishing or enforcing "house rules" with a child's friend because the way in which they speak to their child is not the same as the way they would speak to another person's child. In fact, many parents use the "nag, then yell" technique for enforcing rules with their own children. It goes something like this: *"Pick up your games before you get something else out. I said, pick up your games before you take out your chemistry set. Are you listening to me? How many times have I told you to put the games away before you get out something else out?* (Then, yelling): *Aren't you ever going to learn? I said pick up your games!!!!!!"* This technique is not one that most parents would feel comfortable using with their children's friends. The loud, angry, tense tone of voice is meant to communicate to their child that they are serious, yet it would be simply rude and inappropriate with another person's child. Often, therefore, parents keep their mouths shut and say nothing at all to the visitor, waiting until the other child leaves, then saddling their own child with the overwhelming task of cleaning up. This is a mistake. In remaining silent, we send the unspoken message to our children that we don't have enough conviction in our values to enforce them across the board. This is not to imply, however, that you should scream and yell at your visitors. Rather, begin by practicing a respectful tone of voice and using respectful words with your own children. You'll probably find that you can get effective results without yelling and being harsh. With a little practice, you'll find that a respectful tone will help you feel more comfortable asking your child's playmate to conform to the rules of the house as well.

Communicate Honestly and Clearly

Many times we believe we're being clear with children when in reality we're not. Saying "I really don't like it when there are too many toys out at a time" tells the child nothing about what you would like her to do about it. An honest, clear communication includes your own feelings and an "I would like you to . . ." statement. If a child drags all the toys in the house out without a thought of putting them back, you might say "I feel uncomfortable with too many toys being out. I would like you to put the Twister game and puzzles away before you play with the Legos." In this statement, you're asking the children to respect your feelings as well as your values. In addition, you're communicating your specific expectations so that there's no guesswork about what behavior you'd like to see.

Use Well-Defined Consequences

Consequences are not punishment; therefore, there is no reason why you cannot use them with a playmate just as you would use them with your own child. Especially in situations where you know a child is likely to get a lot of toys out or break certain rules, often it's helpful to sit down with both children for one minute prior to playing and tell them what the consequences will be if they break any house rule. Be sure when you do this that you clearly define for the children what the house rules are. You might say something like "In this house we only get a few toys out at a time. If I see that too many toys are being taken out, I'm going to ask you to put them back. Then you can either put them back, or we'll take a ten-minute break from playing. Does everyone understand?"

While it may be difficult to conceive of being assertive with your children's friends, many parents tell me that once they've taken the initiative and made the rules clear, it's not uncommon for their children's friends to prefer coming over to play rather than having play dates at their own houses. Children appreciate well-defined boundaries, and if the rules are communicated with respect, you'll not only strengthen your values in your child's eyes, but you'll win the respect of their friends as well.

Part Two

Your Child's Relationships

Chapter 6

"You Can't Make Me!"

Your Relationship with Your Child

The relationship between you and your child is a complex and precious process that began at conception and will continue throughout both of your lives. Often parents ask whether the mistakes they make will "ruin" their children. My answer is this: The way in which you interact with your child, the process that you undergo in building a continuing relationship with him or her, the conscientiousness with which you apply yourself to the process, the mistakes you make, all go into creating the adult your child will become. I realize that's probably not the answer parents are looking for and that it's not terribly satisfying to hear. It's certainly not as satisfying as if I were to say "No, no problem, mistakes don't ruin children," but I do think that it's more accurate.

To imply that our actions, either bad or good, conscious or unconscious, have no effect on our children would be lying. On the other hand, to imply that every little mistake we make with our children has catastrophic implications for their adult life would be ludicrous. As parents, we are similar to an artist creating a painting. How does an artist do that? First, she has an idea of what the finished piece will look like. She chooses her canvas and colors carefully. She balances spontaneity with technique. She steps back every once in a while to determine how it's going and makes adjustments accordingly. If she makes a mistake, does she throw the painting out? Of course not. She contemplates the error. How bad is it? Can she paint over it? Can she work it in to the finished painting? What adjustments must she make in order to wind up with a product similar to her original vision? When I was taking a watercolor class, one of my mentors told me that I was too careful, that in order to create a real masterpiece, I must risk making mistakes, because without the risks and without a few mistakes, my painting would be flat and lifeless. He was right. The best paintings I ever did have some mistakes in them—a splash of color in the "wrong" place, a line that's not perfectly straight. Some mistakes are necessary to create a true masterpiece. Obviously, if you deliberately make mistake after mistake after mistake, without ever stopping to step back and make corrections, you aren't going to wind up with the result that you originally had in mind. But in helping children develop into their full potential, we must realize that we will make some mistakes, and those mistakes will ultimately form our children into unique individuals.

In addition to recognizing that parenting without mistakes isn't possible, we also must recognize that our relationship with our children will not be a completely harmonious one. Like the mistakes that we make, quarrels, tension, and power struggles are part of any relationship. Our focus should be on how we handle these moments rather than whether we can eradicate them.

The Birth and Development of the Power Struggle

There isn't a parent in the world who hasn't, at one time or another, found himself locked in mortal combat with a child, struggling for power. From the minute a child can pronounce the word "no" straight through and including adulthood, parents find the notion of power—what kind of power, how much power, and when to give power to a child—a frustrating and sometimes over-whelming challenge.

When our children are infants, power is not an issue. For one thing, they can't talk back; for another, they are so small that we easily dominate them. We, the parents, have the power in the re-lationship. No ifs, ands, or buts. Or do we?

Who determines when the infant eats; who has the power there? Well, the infant. How about who determines when the in-fant sleeps; who has the power there? Again, the infant. Who de-termines when the infant plays or is picked up? At least for the infants whose parents are trying to be attuned to their baby's needs, again the answer would be . . . the infant. Maybe the rea-son that we think we have the power when our children are in-fants is because it seems so natural. Maybe it's simply the *struggle* for power that doesn't exist at that stage. It seems natural that we should feed the baby when he's hungry, let her sleep when she's tired, play with him or pick him up when he cries. And when things seem natural, there is a give-and-take, a flow of power that shifts back and forth between parent and baby.

Then infants become toddlers. They're still small enough for us to dominate them physically, but suddenly they're mobile—and *fast!* For their safety, limits must be set. Those limits are generally set with the word "no." Who has the power when the word "no" is used? Well, the user. In this case, the adult. "No, honey, don't touch that." "Hey, get out of there, that's a no-no." "I said 'no'!" Powerful statements using powerful words. Mom or Dad has the power. The "flow" of power that felt so natural during infancy dis-appears.

Then the toddler learns to talk. If you surveyed 100 parents and asked them what their child's first word was, I would con-servatively estimate that at least fifty would say the word was "no." And the remaining fifty would name the word "no" when asked to list the child's first ten words. "Honey, it's time to eat." "NO!" "Nap time, come on let's go." "NO!" "Time to go bye-bye."

"NO!" *Voilà!* The power struggle is born. From this time forward it seems as if life becomes a series of struggles over who is in control. Many times the issue in itself is not being fought over, it's the *power* that each side really wants. But things aren't all bad. At least for the parents of most toddlers, the final point is moot—after all, you can always physically overpower a toddler.

Then elementary school arrives. Your child is no longer physically small enough for you to dominate him easily. Suddenly there is more at stake when you engage in a power struggle with your child. After all, what happens if your child says "No, you can't make me?" and you know that you really can't? It seems that one thing some parents rely on is that a power struggle simply won't occur. After all, power struggles don't really dominate our lives with our children, do they? I mean, there are those moments when you say "Time to put your coat on" and your child says "Okay." Or you say "You know, hon, I really don't want you to go to the movies with your friends tonight. Aunt Martha's coming to dinner." And your child replies "Well, okay, I'll go another night." "Wow," you think, "If only it could always be that easy!" And you sigh with relief.

So frankly, it is a surprise when your child doesn't engage in a power struggle with you. But why the surprise? It's obvious that when our needs and wishes are attuned with our child's needs and wishes, the natural flow of power that occurred during infancy returns.

True, you're probably thinking, but how often do the needs and wishes of the adults coincide so neatly with the needs and wishes of the children? Not very often. Not very often, at least, unless you're set up for success.

Setting Yourself Up for Success

Setting yourself up for success means engendering a spirit of cooperation between you and your child. Cooperation means working together with one or more other people so that there is a common benefit. If people are working together toward a common goal, they are more likely to be attuned to each other. With attunement and cooperation, the flow of power between you and your child will return, and power struggles will diminish.

Creating an Atmosphere Where Cooperation Thrives

The foundation of a cooperative relationship lies in the concept and practice of mutual respect. In order to create this atmosphere, we must first recognize that our children are equal to us in many ways.

"Equal? You've got to be kidding! My kid doesn't have the experience and knowledge that I have. He doesn't know how the world works. I'm his superior, there's no doubt about it."

This father's attitude is typical. Please don't misunderstand me. There are many ways in which our children are different from us. They do have less experience and knowledge. They're also shorter, younger, more energetic, and far more innocent. It's important to recognize and remember that the ways in which we're different from our children make us responsible for protecting and instructing them. But there are equalities too—fundamental ways in which our children don't differ from us. For one thing, they're human beings, with needs and rights like all human beings. Not only do they have similar physical needs—to eat, sleep, wash, and so on—but they have similar emotional needs as well. Children, like adults, have the need to feel protected, the need for love, the need to feel listened to and understood, the need to feel in control, the need to be alone sometimes. The similarities or equalities between parents and children are what classify us all as human. And all human beings deserve to be treated in a respectful way.

The Paradox of Parenting

Our children are the most important things in the world to us. In fact, the thought of losing a child sends chills down most parents' spines. When we read in the news about a child being abducted, or children who have fatal illnesses or were brutally murdered, we all feel a momentary chill of fear, perhaps mentally checking "Where are my kids right now? Are they safe?" and then breathing a sigh of relief. "Yes, the kids are safe. Everything is okay." For most parents, the thought of losing a child is akin to losing one's own arm or leg. And truthfully, I think most parents, if they had to make a choice, would gladly say "Take my arm. But don't take my child."

A number of years ago the twelve-year-old daughter of our friends died. Her death devastated her family, it devastated her friends, and it devastated her neighbors. We mourned for and with them that day and for many weeks afterward. The mourning has never quite left any of us. And we, their friends and neighbors, held our children a little closer after that because the thought of ever losing our own children was unbearable.

And that brings me to the paradox of parenting. Even though we love our children more than anything else in the whole world, even though we can't bear the thought that we might ever lose them, even though they are more precious to us than gold, there are times when we treat them in ways that we wouldn't treat a stranger on the street.

Respecting your children means treating them like the gifts they are.

The Three Questions

In order to determine whether you're treating your children with respect, I used to tell parents to reflect on one question. Later I decided that they should reflect on three questions instead. The first question I tell parents to ask themselves (and it used to be the only question) is: "Would you treat your spouse this way?" (You probably can see why this was problematic if it was the only question you had to answer. Often I got a response of "Yes, I treat my spouse this way all the time!") So the next question is: "Would I treat my best friend this way?" and the third question is: "Would I want to be treated this way?" If you answered "no" to any of these three questions, then you're not treating your child with respect.

Treating children respectfully doesn't mean allowing them to get away with misbehaving. Discipline is an important component of raising a child. But it is possible to discipline and act respectful at the same time. Keep in mind that no one is willing to listen to another side if he doesn't feel respected. By treating your children with respect, you set them up to listen when you feel your point of view matters. This diminishes power struggles and cooperation grows from this foundation.

The Need for Power

As human beings, we all have a need for power. Having power over certain situations gives us a sense of control and satisfaction and contributes to high self-esteem. Children also need appropriate power, and as parents, if we fail to give them power, they'll find a way to take it.

"Ever since my child was a toddler, I just felt she had no sense of style or color coordination. So I always insisted in choosing her outfits for her. Even when she kicked up a terrible fuss, I always won. When she got into elementary school things were fine for a while, but then I noticed that she was almost too subservient. Her backpack always seemed stuffed full with schoolwork, and one day I decided that I'd see if I could consolidate things for her. When I took out her notebooks, I noticed that there was an outfit stuffed in the bottom of her bag. Apparently, she

had been taking an alternate set of clothes with her to school, changing in the bathroom, and then changing back immediately before coming home. I realized at that point that I had been too controlling, that it was so bad that my child would break the trust I thought we had in the relationship."

As this mother discovered, if children aren't given appropriate power at appropriate ages, they'll simply take it. It's clear that the consequences reach far beyond the behavior, for many times the taking of power means you must lie to the people you trust, whether it is a lie of omission or a blatant lie. The lying eats away at a child's relationship with his parents, which ultimately is not worth the short-term control you might achieve.

Determining Where Power Belongs

Many parents fall into the trap of believing that simply because they're the adults, all the power automatically belongs to them. Sometimes this *is* the case—as in situations where you must protect your child—and sometimes it's *not* the case, as in situations where your child is responsible for his own bodily functions. If the power should belong to your child and you take it away, albeit respectfully, your child will run into difficulty.

Clearly there will be times when the division of power is foggy, but there are also many situations in which the power is (or at least should be) clear-cut. For example, when the issue has to do with control over someone's body or bodily functions, the majority of the power should belong to that person. Eating, sleeping, going to the bathroom, and getting dressed are good examples. These are things that elementary school children can be given some control over. Specifically, while you are still in charge of having healthful food in the house, the child of elementary school age can be given the responsibility of deciding how much or even if she wants to eat. While you can still decide at what hour your child should be in bed, he can be given input into the decision and ultimately should be responsible for falling asleep and taking care of his middle-of-the-night needs (such as going to the bathroom or getting a drink of water) himself. Many parents still find themselves in the middle of power struggles over going to the bathroom. Again, this is something that your child can be gently reminded to do prior to leaving the house, but ultimately it should be something for which the decision rests in her hands. Choosing appropriate clothing and getting dressed are other areas where your child's independence can be stimulated. If you find yourself in a power struggle over issues of this type, remember that your ultimate goal is to release responsibility to your child so that he can develop the resources to handle these things independently.

To help you determine if you're giving appropriate power to your child, ask yourself these questions:

- Are the limits you're setting hindering the goal of developing your child's independence?
- Are the limits you're setting age appropriate? What are most other people's children this age able to do for themselves?
- Do you find yourself in frequent power struggles over a particular issue?
- What is the worst that could happen if you allowed your child to have the power?

No Permissive Parents

Allowing your children to have some power doesn't mean being permissive and letting them run the show. Clearly, as the adult, you have the responsibility of keeping your children safe and teaching them about the world. You also have the obligation to set the limits that give your child a sense of safety and security.

But power is not necessarily a black-and-white issue. In most things, there is a division of power. One thing you can do to satisfy your child's need for power without becoming a permissive parent is to offer power in the form of choices appropriate for the child's developmental level.

"It seems like my six-year-old daughter and I were always in power struggles over which television programs she could watch. In thinking about the division of responsibility, I decided that I should be responsible for the length of time she could watch and which channels she could watch freely, but then she could make her own choices after that. So we discussed it, and I told her which two channels I thought that she could choose freely from and that she could watch one hour a day. But I told her she would be responsible for deciding which hour (or which two half hours) and what she wanted to watch during that time. I also said that if there was a special program on another channel, she could watch it if she cleared it with me first. You can't believe how enthusiastically she responded! Since then she gets out the *TV Guide* and plans her program watching on a daily basis. Our power struggles really ended after that."

This mom did a great job dividing the power about television. In giving some power to her daughter, she satisfied the girl's need. As her daughter gets older, the freedom needs to expand. Remember that the rule of thumb is "Little choices for little people, big choices for big people." Therefore, a five-year-old child should be offered smaller choices than an eight-year-old, and an eight-year-old smaller choices than a ten-year-old. The choices you offer your child will be based not only on the child's developmental level but also on your values. The key lies in remembering that there are always choices within whatever limits you might set.

Remember, too, that if your children are feeling discouraged about power and they're rebelling, it does not mean that you must relinquish power on the issue that's being rebelled against. What you should do, however, is reexamine the whole picture. Ask yourself if the power really belongs to you in this particular instance. If it does, look for other areas where the reins might be too tight and loosen them a bit. Remember that power is something all human beings need to be healthy, and look for areas where your children can feel a sense of satisfaction in this area.

Giving Power Through Family Meetings

Another thing you can do to give power to your child is to allow your child input into the choices the family makes in the context of a family meeting. Decisions about where to go, what to do, and with whom can be discussed in the context of what's best not only for the individual but for the family as well. While your child won't get her way every time, just having her voice heard and respected will help her feel as if her contributions are important; she will feel powerful.

"For easily two years, my eight-year-old has been begging to have a dog. Not only do we already have a cat, but we live in a small apartment. Having a dog really isn't feasible for us. He's been bringing it up at family meetings this whole time. Well, recently, I'd say the past six months, he's shown a lot more responsibility with school and around the house. He does all his homework at the beginning of the week without being asked. He practices his piano every night—again without being asked. He even helps with cleanup in an enthusiastic way. At the last family meeting, he said he had something important to discuss. He presented us with a list of pets he'd like to have and said that he really felt he could be responsible for caring for an animal all by himself. He also presented a reasonable plan for saving his own money to buy a pet and asked if we'd consider it. I was impressed! For the first time I felt that the request and plan seemed sensible. My husband and I told him we'd get back to him at the next meeting. While we still didn't agree to a dog, we told him he could have a guinea pig, and he was thrilled! All talk of a dog stopped, and it was clear that he felt powerful—not only confident and capable of developing a plan, but also that he'd been taken seriously by us."

You're Not at War

Because power is something we all need, it's natural that every family will have issues over power at some point. But a power struggle is not a war. So rather than going armed into battle when a power struggle begins, withdraw your weapons and look at it from a negotiator's or mediator's standpoint. Your job should be to analyze the situation as impartially as possible so that both sides get heard and discussed. And remember that a war can't occur if only one person is fighting.

"I told my daughter that the morning routine wasn't working because she was watching TV instead of getting ready. I said that when she'd finished getting ready, then she could watch TV. She looked at me full in the face and said, 'Well, I'll just turn the TV on when you're not looking!' Boy, did that make me mad, so I said, 'Well, if you do that, then I'll disconnect it.' And she replied with 'Well, then, I'll reconnect it.' Well, now I was boiling, so I went over to the TV and disconnected the cable. And do you know that when I left the room, she reconnected it. I'm furious with her. How can I win?"

When something like this happens, it's important to refrain from verbally engaging your child. This is a classic example of a child pushing to see what happens. Your pushing back usually will result in a power struggle. Try this exercise: Have someone hold a hand up, palm toward you. Put your palm directly on the person's and push. What happens? Ninety-nine percent of the time, the person will push back. Pushing back at your child encourages her to keep pushing. What could this mother have done instead? As bewildering as it may seem, she could have ignored her daughter's remark. If her daughter did indeed turn the TV on when she left the room, she could simply have come in and at that point said, "Well, I see you've chosen to have me disconnect the TV," and refrained from any verbal struggle. If the daughter reconnected it, Mom could have said, "Well, I see you've chosen to have me call the cable company and turn off the cable for a while," then taken action when her daughter was in school. Engaging in verbal battle causes the child to take a position that she is unlikely to want to give up later, because it will mean "losing face." Taking action is always far more powerful in the long run than getting in an argument.

"You Can't Make Me!"

"The other day it was time to go to school, and my son really didn't want to go. We got into a big battle about it, and finally he looked at me defiantly and said, 'I'm not going and you can't make me!' I just felt so helpless, because he was right. At nine years old, I really can't make him! I didn't know what to do."

"You can't make me" is a challenge issued by children who know that it creates feelings of helplessness in their parents. Seeing that look of helplessness on a parent's face or engaging a parent in a verbal or physical struggle is a big payoff for a child who's feeling discouraged about power. Just think about it: Here's this elementary school kid, and all he said was four words—"you can't make me"—and he's got Dad so upset that he's hyperventilating, screaming, or throwing up his hands in despair. Is that powerful or what! When your child says "You can't make me," the best response is to agree: "You're right, I can't make you." This response is the verbal equivalent of letting go of one end of a rope during a game of tug-of-war. It can then be followed with "So, how can we cooperate to work this out?"

"My daughter, who's nine, pulled that on me the other day. But when I asked her how we could cooperate to work it out, she said, 'We can't!' "

While it's always good to begin with the assumption that your child will cooperate (hence the question "How can we cooperate to work this out?"), if your child refuses to cooperate, as this nine-year-old did, it is time to impose some logically related consequences. While you may not be able to make your child go to school, you can give her consequences for staying home—for example, she can stay home but won't be able to watch television. Or she can stay home, but she'll have to pay for the baby-sitter out of her allowance. Sometimes the best lessons aren't learned when children are forced to bend to their parent's will at the moment but rather when they experience the consequences of being uncooperative.

Chapter 7

"I Hate You!"

My eight-year-old daughter was watching me try on clothes in the dressing room of a clothing store. I had tried on several pairs of jeans, none of which fit right, and was feeling exasperated. I sighed. "Em," I said, "I can't wait for you to be old enough to go out and get different sizes for me from the saleslady." She looked up at me, frowned, and calmly stated "I hate you, Mom." Lovely.

When our children say they hate us, when they wish they had different parents, when they scream obscenities at us, these are the moments when most parents wonder why in the world they ever chose to have a child in the first place. These hurtful words evoke feelings that range from sadness to blind rage. Likewise our responses vary depending on what feelings come up for us. Sometimes we say "I hate you too"; other times we turn a cold shoulder, remarking "I don't care if you hate me, you'll do as I say because I'm your mother/father." In truth, very few of our responses are much more effective than if we were to use the old "Sticks and stones may break my bones . . ." and stick out our tongues for good measure.

Why It Hurts So Much

Our sensitivity to our children's rudeness, especially when it's directed at us, is probably due in part to the intensity of our feelings about being a parent. We feel the burden of responsibility to raise our children properly, we love them intensely, many times we feel drained of every last ounce of energy because of how much we give to them. We worry, "Can I protect her?" We feel deep guilt: "I know I screwed up that time." We're insecure about how well we're doing, or if we're doing anything right at all. I remember during a particularly difficult stage with my daughter, at the end of an extremely long day (which had been preceded by an extremely long and difficult night), my husband saying emphatically "I deserve a medal. Parents deserve medals. Someone ought to knock on that door right now and give me one."

I think he's right. Parents need to be recognized for their hard work in some way. The problem is that when you expect that recognition and gratitude to come from your child and it's met head-on by her stating that she hates you (clearly one of the most ungrateful statements I can think of!), it becomes a painful experience.

Single and Adoptive Parents

Single parents and adoptive parents may be especially sensitive about their children's rudeness. In an advanced workshop I was teaching, one single mother, who had adopted her daughter, related this story.

"It was the end of a long day at work, and all I could think about was getting home to Rebecca. I really looked forward to seeing her. Well, maybe I set myself up to be disappointed, but the minute I walked in the door, we started arguing. First she didn't want to do her homework, then she didn't like what we were having for dinner. It seemed like every time I said 'black,' she said 'white,' and then if I said 'Okay, it's white, she'd say 'No it isn't, it's black.' Finally I'd had enough. I told her that since we couldn't get along, I was going to go into my room for a while to be by myself. And you know what she said? She said, 'You're a lousy mother, you know. I wish I had a daddy instead of you.' "

As the mother retold this story, she began to cry. My heart went out to her. How many of us have felt the very same way? For this mother, all the hard work of single parenting, combined with her occasional feelings of anxiety about whether she'd done the right thing in adopting her daughter, some guilt about not "providing her daughter" with a father, and her very natural worries about being an adequate mother all came rushing up at the same time, and she felt overwhelmed with hurt and sadness.

The Truth About Rudeness

When our feelings—either about our parenting skills or about anything else, for that matter—are near the surface, sometimes it's difficult to see the truth about rude behavior—that it may not be rudeness at all but an inappropriate, immature expression of our children's negative feelings.

Just like us, our children have feelings of insecurity, anger, guilt, sadness. Often these negative feelings are difficult for them to express. Imagine, for a moment, a different reply on my daughter's part when we were in the clothing store. Imagine if after I said, "I can't wait for you to be old enough to go out and get different sizes for me from the saleslady," my daughter had said "Gee, Mom, that hurts my feelings. I feel old enough now to ask the saleslady for a different size for you. I wish you would be more careful in your estimation of my burgeoning independence and competence."

Okay, it's a laugh, right? It sounds ridiculous to suggest that even an adult might be able to identify and clearly state feelings in this way, much less an eight-year-old child. Yet if she could have stated distinctly what her feelings and thoughts were at the time, this probably would come close. As it was, "I hate you" was the only thing she could think of to say that would not only capture my attention but would come close to the angry, frustrated, and hurt feelings she was having.

When Your Child Uses Foul Language

"Okay, maybe I can ignore it when my child says he hates me, because he's just not expressing himself clearly, but what do I do when he calls me a bitch?"

For most parents, it's easier to recognize a child's negative feelings when the expression of those feelings is relatively mild ("I hate you") than when it's more forceful ("You're a bitch"). But neither of these cases calls for us to ignore our children and go about our business as if we hadn't heard them.

It's Not About Turning a Deaf Ear . . .

As parents, there are very few circumstances in which we should not take some sort of action. Children need parents to provide leadership, exhibit decision-making skills, and teach them about the ways of the world and, perhaps more important, about the morals and ethics that we uphold in our family. In essence, we have to be aware and proactive about the messages, both verbal and nonverbal, overt and covert, that we send to our children. When we ignore the words "I hate you," or "You're a lousy mother," or "You're a bitch," we send the wrong message to the child. The child may get the idea that it's okay to name-call and to express negative feelings in hurtful ways. Just as you would stop your children from physically hurting you, you also must stop your children from verbally hurting you.

The key to stopping these kinds of hurtful words first requires that we help our children understand that although they have power, they lack clarity and are, therefore, pretty useless.

. . . It's About Diminishing the Power

One of the reasons why children are so attracted to foul language and hateful words is that they feel powerful. Children are often lacking in power because of their status in the household, and using these expressions makes them feel strong and more adult-like. But why do these words feel so powerful? Why doesn't "rats!" have the same zing as "shit!" when we stub a toe? Why don't we say "fudge" instead of . . . well, you know the word I mean. The answer, I believe, lies in our reaction to these four-letter words. Children know that these words shock and dismay us. They know that adults get red in the face, flustered, and embarrassed when one of these words is used. They also may know that Mom or Dad might have a tendency to use these words when she or he is really, really mad. In addition, society reacts much the same as Mom or Dad, which serves to reinforce the power of these words for our children.

But how do we take the power out of these words? What is a different message that we can send to our children?

Refuse to Be Hurt

The first step in disempowering four-letter words (including "hate") requires that we refuse to be hurt, shocked, or angry. Because the power in these words lies in their ability to evoke these feelings, children are likely to use them for that purpose. If you refuse to be hurt and simply recognize that these are tactics with which your child is trying to get a rise out of you, then when she doesn't get the rise, she won't find this method particularly helpful in the future.

Children Do What Works

One of the most wonderful things about children that I've encountered in the many years I've worked with them and with their parents is that they rarely do things that don't work. If your child calls you a "bitch" or says "I hate you" on a regular basis, then he must be getting something out of it. Think to yourself "What's the payoff here?" "How is this working for my child?" In all likelihood, you'll recognize that the payoff for your child is in your reaction. These words do get your attention and make you angry. Many times simply changing your reaction will change your child's tendency to use these words.

Replacing Your Reaction

Once you've decided not to pay off your child for using four-letter words, it's time to think about the next step. Simply not reacting would be too similar to "ignoring," which we already know isn't appropriate.

Because one of our goals as parents is to teach our children how to express their feelings in socially appropriate ways, the next step must focus on feelings. When your child uses a four-letter word, what is she feeling? Is she angry at you? Feeling ignored or misunderstood? Feeling playful and trying to tease? A member of one of my groups said:

"I have a problem. My son has started to use the word 'damn.' He uses it very appropriately, like if I tell him that he has to put his toys away and come to the table, he'll say 'damn,' almost under his breath. And then he does what I've asked. It's not as if he's angry. If it only happened once in a while, I guess I might just hope it would go away, but the problem is that there are at least ten times during the day when it seems to serve as an appropriate exclamation for him. I've tried ignoring it, but it isn't going away."

Handling Feelings First

Here is a situation where Mom needs to give a little thought about the feelings behind the exclamation. Clearly the word feels powerful to her son, or he wouldn't use it. But his payoff isn't coming from Mom's reaction, because she hasn't been reacting. So let's take the feelings first. What is he feeling? Probably disappointed that he has to leave the activity he's engaged in and come to the table. But what's his payoff?

"Well," added his mother, "there's another boy at school that he admires a great deal. I know that the other boy uses these words, and I think my son has picked up on it."

Aha! The payoffs that come from peers are often as strong, if not stronger, than the payoffs we provide. Since Mom can't change her son's payoff, her job will be to give him more appropriate words to express himself by saying something like "You seem disappointed about having to leave what you're doing."

Teaching the Right Lesson at the Wrong Time

"Wait a minute! When my daughter uses four-letter words, it's because she's angry. And I'm not going to stand by when she calls her mother a 'bitch' and say something wimpy like 'You sound angry.' She can't talk to my wife that way, and she's gonna hear from me about it. I'm gonna teach her a lesson."

There are many times when we need to teach our children lessons about right and wrong. Because using curse words is wrong, a lesson does indeed need to be taught. The key, however, lies in the timing of the lesson. This irate father clearly wants to teach his daughter a lesson *now,* when she's using angry words. But think for a moment. In order to learn a lesson, what has to happen? Well, first we have to be able to listen to the lesson that's being taught. We have to feel receptive and open to hearing what the teacher has to say. We need to feel respectful enough toward the teacher to recognize that the lesson is valuable and should be retained. We need to be willing to act upon the lesson that was taught. This dad has the right idea. Teaching his daughter that swear words are inappropriate is the right lesson, but he's trying to teach it at the wrong time.

Choosing the Right Time for the Lesson

Children—in fact, human beings of all ages—learn best when they're relaxed, when there are no distractions, and when their feelings are not intense. For us, this means that in order to teach our children lessons about right and wrong, we must deliberately set up time to converse with them about certain topics. We're not angry and neither are they. Nobody's eating, or watching television, or trying to get homework done. This is special time set aside for learning.

Imparting the Lesson

"I went back to my son and talked to him about using the word 'damn.' I waited until right before bed, because he's the most relaxed then and we usually have good conversations about all kinds of things at that time of the day. I told him that I'd noticed he was using the word 'damn' a lot and that I felt confused when he used it. He looked at me in a very puzzled way. To tell you the truth, I think he was surprised that I'd even noticed. I think he was even more surprised to hear me use it casually, because he's never heard me swear before. But I could tell he was still listening. So I said, 'I'm a little confused when you use it, because it doesn't really tell me how you feel. I know you're having feelings, but when I don't know what those feelings are, I really don't know how to help you with them. I was wondering if we could think together about words that are more descriptive than "damn" and would better tell me what you're feeling.' I kind of shrugged my shoulders when I said it, trying to act like the word itself didn't really effect me so I wouldn't 'pay him off.' Well, I was surprised because I really didn't think he'd respond. But he did! Together we came up with some words like disappointed, sad, frustrated. His reaction was like 'Okay, Mommy, I'll use those words instead.' "

This is a great example of teaching the right lesson at the right time. Without paying off her child for using swear words, and without lecturing, Mom helped her son come up with words that were clearer and more concise than the one he'd been using. She said with her words as well as with her reaction that "damn" confused her rather than made her angry, and in essence communicated to her son the question "How can we clear up my confusion?" In addition, her attitude of respect helped put her son at ease and made him more receptive to learning the lesson she was trying to impart.

It's important to understand that this wasn't the last time that her son used "damn." But thereafter, when she heard the word, Mom was able to say "I guess you're trying to tell me something about your feelings. You seem disappointed (or angry, or frustrated, etc)." Eventually her son stopped using the word altogether.

When Your Child Is Rude to Others

"What happens when my son says 'I don't like you, you're ugly' to his grandmother? I mean, she's from the old school, and frankly, I feel mortified."

"My daughter responds that way when people talk to her on the street or in the elevator in our building. Sometimes she even sticks out her tongue when she says it. I'm at my wit's end."

Public situations are often the most difficult for parents. At these times, our own feelings of embarrassment, anger, disappointment, rush up and crowd out even the best-learned techniques.

Why Do Our Children Act This Way?

Many times our children behave rudely in public because they're uncomfortable in the situation. Maybe Grandma pinches your daughter's cheeks too hard, maybe strangers intimidate your son when they stick their faces so close to his. Remember that your primary responsibility at the moment the rudeness occurs is to figure out how your child is feeling and communicate those feelings back to him or her. You might say to your son or daughter, in front of Grandma, "Seems like you're feeling a little uncomfortable. Sometimes it's hard to figure out how to tell people your feelings." Not only will this serve to model the kind of language children should use when they do feel uncomfortable, but it will communicate to Grandma or the strangers that the behavior isn't intentionally rude, just a miscommunication. Again, it's important to teach the lesson later, at a better time when your child will be receptive.

Giving Your Child Alternatives

Sometimes it's not enough for a child to be able to express her feelings differently. After all, it might not be appropriate for him to say "I feel uncomfortable around Grandma" in front of her! When you're discussing this with your child after Grandma's gone home, you might consider asking if he can think of something that would help him feel more comfortable when Grandma comes, or tell him that he's welcome to express his thoughts about Grandma to you privately after she leaves. By giving him a voice, even if he has to express himself later, you'll give him the freedom to refrain from being rude.

Be a Role Model—What Kinds of Words Do You Use?

Finally, it's important that we not underestimate a child's need to model the behavior of his parents. When children hear their parents swearing like sailors, it's likely that they'll swear like sailors too. It's difficult to teach a lesson when you've adopted a "do as I say, not as I do" philosophy. You don't have to be a saint, but cutting down on your own use of these words will help your child in ways that "lessons" never will.

Are You Feeling Resistant?

When we were discussing this topic in a group I was facilitating, one father shook his head and said, "I'm sorry, but when my child calls my wife names, I just see red. I really don't think that all this is going to help. If I don't teach her right then and there, I just know she's going to get the impression that it's okay and I can't have that."

Another group member leaned over and said, "Let me ask you a question. How have you been handling it?"

"Well, I send her to her room!" he replied. "And sometimes I raise my voice and tell her that she is not allowed to behave like that in my house."

"And has that worked?" the other member asked. "Has she stopped calling your wife names?"

"Well, no . . ." was the reply.

Sometimes It's Hard to Change

It's understandable to want to resist new ways of doing things. It's hard to change, for one thing, and the old ways just seem so much easier most of the time. Changing means thinking hard not only before we act but as we're acting. Our old ways are more comfortable and, clearly, in this father's case, at least allowed him to vent his own feelings of discomfort and anger.

The most important question to ask yourself when you find yourself resistant to trying something new is "Is what I'm doing now working?" If it's not, then it seems to me you have nothing to lose by trying something else.

Chapter 8

"My Child Never Listens, No Matter How Much I Nag!"

I nag and I nag and I nag. He just doesn't listen. For example, I tell him to turn off the TV, it's time to do his homework. No response. So I say it again. He still doesn't respond. Sometimes I repeat myself a half a dozen times. Finally I stand in front of the TV and scream at him and he looks up and says 'Huh?' And you know what really gets me? That *he's* annoyed because I interrupted his program and yelled at him."

Sound familiar? There are few things more annoying to parents than when a child doesn't listen. We begin by asking nicely. It's usually a reasonable request and not necessarily one that would even take that much effort on the child's part. But we get no response. As we repeat ourselves, we begin to feel more and more angry, out of control, insulted, and disrespected. Ultimately, we explode at our child and she is finally motivated enough to do what we've asked. One parent told me that she deliberately raises her voice, because that's the only thing that seems to "work" with her daughter.

Why Yelling Works and Why You Still Shouldn't Do It

There's a very good reason why yelling works. It works because your raised voice and harsh words serve as the child's *cue* to listen. Children tune out nagging because they know they don't have to listen yet. Then when you raise your voice, your child tunes back in because he knows the nagging is over and it's time for business. In other words, parents who nag, then yell, have conditioned their children to respond only to the yelling. In order to teach your child to listen, you have to have a different "cue" that will send the signal that you mean business. This "cue" will teach your child not only to listen but also to take responsibility for turning off the TV, doing his homework, picking up his toys, or whatever it is you're asking of him.

Replacing the "Cue"

One of the most effective replacements for the "cue" of yelling that I know of is the "I" message. "I" messages serve as an explanation to the child of what behavior you dislike and why, and what you'd like your child to do differently. There are many different ways of giving "I" messages to children, but the one I find to be the most effective has four parts and is borrowed from Michael Popkin's *Active Parenting* book and workshop. It sounds like this:

> <u>When you</u> watch TV and ignore me
> <u>I feel</u> frustrated
> <u>Because</u> the TV seems more important than I am.
> <u>I would like you to</u> respond when I speak to you.

Because the "I" message is repetitive and the child gets used to hearing it for various misbehaviors, it ultimately replaces the old cue. Many times children, upon hearing the words "When you . . ." will say "Okay, okay, I'm doing it."

You've Got to Be Kidding!

Actually, I'm not kidding, but it's true that whenever I teach "I" messages to groups, I invariably get incredulous looks and comments.

"You mean my kid is going to listen just because I say 'When you _____, I feel _____, Because _____ and I would like you to _____?' You've got to be kidding! I've reasoned, I've yelled, I've punished, and none of that worked. Why is this going to work any better? What makes you so sure that he won't just tune this out too?"

"I" messages work surprisingly well by themselves, and I recommend that you suspend your disbelief and try them. However, it is true that children who are used to ignoring parents often have their nonlistening technique down to a science. Some kids are so good at tuning out that a hurricane could blow the house down around them and they'd never know it. Thus, sometimes it's necessary to follow an "I" message with action. We've already talked about taking effective action by offering children choices that have consequences attached. (See Chapters 1, 3, and 5 for examples.) Offering your child a choice following your "I" message (whether you believe she's listening or not) then acting on the choice will teach her to listen to the "I" message more closely next time.

Added Benefits

"I" messages help our children in a variety of ways that reach beyond simply correcting misbehavior or replacing cues to listen.

They also help children internalize the values that we hold so dear and upon which our rules or requests are based. Research indicates that children need an explanation in order to internalize a message. The problem is that most parents confuse explanation with reasoning.

The Difficulty with Reasoning

"My nine-year-old encourages my two-and-a-half-year-old to do dangerous things. For example, even though I've told him again and again how dangerous it is to jump on the bed with the baby, he still does it. I've sat him down and told him about all the things that could happen—some of which are no longer theory! I've even had him repeat it back to me to make sure he heard me. He always says 'Okay, I understand, I won't do it again,' but it could be five minutes, five hours, or five days later, and he's back at it. He just doesn't listen."

Reasoning with children occurs when we attempt to use adult logic as a persuasive device for motivating children to behave in a particular way. The problem is that it simply doesn't work most of the time. When this mother reasons with her nine-year-old and projects about all the possible disasters that might occur, he simply tunes her out. Although he gives the appearance of being reasonable, because he repeats back what she says and agrees with her, he is a child, and as a child, he simply cannot reason in the same way that his mother does. *Children can't reason like adults until they become adults.* Thus, reasoning is a virtually useless tool for most parents. "I" messages, on the other hand, are a concise explanation that, because of their repetitive nature, not only encourage a child to "tune you in" but also provide the explanation necessary for them to internalize the "why" part of your rules.

A Nag Is a Nag Is a Nag . . .

"The other day, my daughter left her puzzle in the middle of the hallway. I asked her to pick it up, but she didn't budge. So I decided to try an 'I' message and said, 'When you leave the puzzle in the middle of the hallway, I feel annoyed because I have to keep stepping over it. I would like for you to pick it up and put it away.' But when I came back, the puzzle was still there. I guess she didn't hear me, so I gave her another 'I' message, but when I came back, it was still there. So I looked her in the face and gave her another 'I' message, but she still didn't move. What will it take to get this kid to listen?"

"I" messages can easily replace the nagging that parents used to use. Repeating yourself over and over, whether what you're repeating is the "I" message or something else entirely, will only excuse your child from listening. If you want your child to listen the first time, you must give the "I" message only once, offer a choice immediately, and if there's still no response, then act on the choice. When this mother's daughter didn't respond after her first "I" message, she could have said "Either pick up the puzzle, or I'll take it apart and put it back in the box, you decide." If the daughter still didn't respond, Mom should simply say "I see you've decided to have me put the puzzle away," then proceed to do so, despite any wailing and carrying on that the daughter might do.

Why Children Wail

The wailing and carrying on that children do are often a way for them to test and see if you'll change your mind. After all, children would rather not have to listen. But if you stay firm and simply say "It seems as if you're unhappy with this choice. Maybe next time you'll listen when I ask you to do something and make a choice sooner so that I don't have to make the choice for you," you'll see that eventually she will calm down, and you'll be one step closer to teaching her the listening skills she needs to thrive in life.

Another reason that children get upset once you impose a consequence is that they're genuinely sorry.

"I told my son that if he didn't clean up the mess he'd made in the living room I'd put it away myself, but then he wouldn't be able to have it for a day. It was his favorite—a microscope kit. When he didn't respond after the 'I' message and choice, I did take it away. But then he cried. And I could tell he was genuinely sorry he'd made that choice. I didn't know if I should give it back to him or not."

This is a dilemma that many parents face. Sometimes our children are genuinely sorry for their actions, so it's tough to stick with the consequences we've set up. As your child's parent, you'll need to make the decision about whether he's learned his lesson on a case-by-case basis. Remember, though, that when our children struggle with the choices they've made, they often benefit. So, while I don't want to seem rigid, it really is okay to allow your child to struggle with the consequences of his actions. I'm reminded of the story about a teacher who sent his student into the woods to watch a butterfly emerging from its cocoon. The student waited patiently as he watched the butterfly struggle to free itself. Finally the student's heart was filled with compassion for the poor butterfly, and, ever so gently, he reached in and helped the butterfly out of the cocoon. The butterfly flew a few feet, then fell to the ground and died. The student began to cry, and he ran back to his teacher and asked, "Why? Why did the butterfly die?" The teacher replied, "When you reached in and helped the butterfly out of its cocoon, you deprived it of the opportunity to strengthen its wings in the struggle."*

*Michael Popkin, *Active Parenting: All Video Series*. Marietta, Ga.: Active Parenting Publishers.

When you allow your children to struggle with the consequences of their actions, you're giving them the opportunity to strengthen their wings. Ultimately, your children will fly higher and faster and farther because they've strengthened their wings in the struggle.

What If My Kid Doesn't Care?

"The other day my daughter left about three pairs of shoes in various places all over the house. I gave her an 'I' message and said, 'When you leave your shoes all over the place, I feel frustrated because I keep tripping over them. I'd like you to put them away.' Of course she didn't, so I said, 'Either put them away, or I'll take them and you'll have to wear a pair you don't like tomorrow.' She still didn't respond, and when I acted, she didn't even seem to care."

One mistake parents make when giving "I" messages and consequences is being fooled by a child's lackadaisical attitude. Sometimes children act as if they don't care as a way to see if that particular tactic will get you to change your mind. But even if a child doesn't respond dramatically to a consequence you've imposed, it's important to remember that it doesn't necessarily mean that she isn't learning from the consequence. Many parents have the mistaken idea that a child needs to feel hurt or upset in order to learn. This is simply a fallacy. In fact, often the subtler, less dramatic consequences work best.

"I could have sworn that my son couldn't have cared less when I told him that he couldn't go to the park with his friends because he hadn't cleaned his room when I'd asked. He simply shrugged his shoulders and disappeared into his room, and within minutes was playing happily. I was very surprised the next week on Saturday morning when I saw him cleaning his room without being asked. I complimented him on it and he said, 'Well,

I figured that I'd better get going if I wanted to get to the park in time to join the baseball game.' "

Just because a child doesn't react immediately when a consequence is imposed, it still can effectively teach the lesson we have in mind.

Second Chances

Sometimes parents feel uncomfortable with the idea of saying things only once, then acting. I frequently hear the refrain: "But don't children deserve another chance? I mean, I want to be patient; saying things only once sounds awfully strict and harsh."

First of all, inherent within the "I" message/choice/consequence sequence are several chances. If you ask once, without giving an "I" message, that's one chance. Giving your child a chance to respond after the "I" message is a second chance. She then has one more chance to act after you offer a choice. So in reality, there are already three chances. While it still may seem as if you're lacking in patience to give only three chances to your child, this kind of patience often has its own difficulties.

The Problem with Patience

The most common definition of "patient" in *Webster's New Collegiate Dictionary* reads: "to bear pains or trials calmly or without complaint." But if we bear our children's misbehavior without complaint, what are we teaching them? In the long run, how effective is our patience? Most parents are patient to a point, and once they reach that point, they explode in anger. What, ultimately, does our child learn when she continuously misbehaves without repercussions and sees us "being patient," only to explode in the end?

"I just don't understand it," one mom complained. "He was so awful all weekend, and I was so patient. I must have bitten my tongue a thousand times, and he just kept at me. Finally I just couldn't take it anymore and I lost it. I felt completely unappreciated."

Many parents believe they're being patient when in reality they're letting their children walk all over them. This kind of patience is detrimental to both parent and child. Biting our tongues or bearing our painful feelings and trials without complaint when our child is misbehaving generally means that we're stuffing our own increasingly negative feelings deep down inside of ourselves where they fester and grow until we can't stand it any more. Finally they explode out of us, causing us to "lose it" with our children.

The "Bell Curve" of Feelings

Jeanne and Don Elium, coauthors of *Raising a Son* and *Raising a Daughter*, suggest that our feelings can be represented in a bell curve. Initially, your feelings about your child's misbehavior may be mildly negative, but as the misbehavior continues, your feelings begin to escalate, rising until they reach a "point of no return." Prior to that point of no return, your thoughts were clear, your patience commendable by most standards. But upon hitting the point of no return, you enter into what they call the "nonthinking zone." While in this zone, your thoughts are muddled, your negative feelings are intense, and you lose not only patience but the capacity for either rational thought or action. Given enough time, of course, your feelings eventually subside, and you again become capable of thinking and acting rationally, and "with patience."

Clearly, this practice serves no one. In fact, when your frustration level is so high, you probably wind up acting more disrespectfully toward your child and being harsher and more punitive than you would have been if you hadn't been "patient" in the first place. In other words, the practice of being patient often undermines its own goal!

Action Has Rewards

When you act rather than "being patient" while your child misbehaves, your action will take place before you reach the point of no return. It is more likely to be based, therefore, on clear, rational thoughts. Your child will not see you as impatient but will view you as a parent who has thought out the limits and rules, and who is in charge. He or she ultimately will respect you for taking a stand early in the misbehavior.

The Benefits of an Early Stand

This early stand benefits the child in many ways. When he feels as if you have a clear idea of what the limits are, he feels more secure in his environment. A parent who is "patient" and then explodes, however, is confusing to a child. He can't see the festering feelings that you have during the time you're being patient, all he sees is that you're letting him get away with a lot of misbehavior. He figures he's home free, until you explode and become a raging lunatic. Then he's likely to feel confused, because "Why was it okay to do this a minute ago, and now it looks like it's a really terrible thing?"

I like Webster's third and fourth definitions of patience better than the most common definition. According to Webster, to be patient also means "not hasty or impetuous; steadfast despite opposition, difficulty or adversity." A parent who is not hasty sets limits based on clear, rational guidelines. She doesn't act impetuously because rather than "being patient" and stuffing her feelings down until they reach astronomical proportions, she acts immediately when limits are called for. This type of "patient parent" is steadfast and firm about the limits she's set, knowing that they're in the child's best interests, and she's willing to be firm about those limits in the face of the child's opposition.

If you become this type of "patient parent," your child will be confident that her parents know what they're doing (at least most of the time) because your words and actions rarely come out of the nonthinking zone. Your child will feel secure and learn for herself how to refrain from acting hastily, how to think through her beliefs and stand up for herself. She will be steadfast about her principles and the other things she believes in. And perhaps most important, she'll never be someone else's "doormat."

Chapter 9

"I'm Scared"

When we moved from our city apartment to a house in the suburbs, my six-year-old daughter seemed fine for a while. Then we decided to enlarge the house. The work took over a year, and during that time, my husband, my daughter, and I were confined to a very small space. When the work was finally finished, my daughter had a beautiful new room upstairs, which she had been really looking forward to. One morning, before she woke up, I took the trash out to the curb. When I turned around, she was standing in the doorway of the house, her face red from crying. 'I couldn't find you! I didn't know where you were,' she screamed at me. And that was when it started. Since then, my daughter won't go upstairs by herself. She has literally become my shadow. And at night it's the worst! She begs and pleads with me to stay by her side because she's afraid. I can't leave the room without her following me."

All children feel afraid sometimes. Sometimes the fear develops suddenly and may be related to a transition of some sort, like moving to a new house, the birth of a sibling, changing schools, divorce. Other times it may seem as if particular children have always been afraid, so much so that fearfulness seems to be part of their personalities.

"My son, who's nine, is very fearful. I guess he's always been that way. Since he was in a 'big boy bed' he's come into our bed at night, claiming he's afraid. And he won't go out into the backyard by himself either. He also insists on turning the lights on in a room before he enters, even if it's daytime. I guess he'll always be afraid."

Still other children may become fearful because of a traumatic experience, such as the death of a loved one or peer.

"We had a terrible experience this year. My eight-year-old son's good friend was killed crossing the street to go to his baseball game. Since then my son has been having terrible separation anxiety and has become very clingy. He's also very fearful: He wants the lights on at night and sometimes comes into our room and sleeps on the floor because he's afraid. I know it's related to his friend's death, but I'm not sure how to help him with it."

Our Response to Fear

Second perhaps only to anger, witnessing the emotion of fear in our children stirs up strong, troubling feelings for us as parents. Primarily, parents respond to fear in one of two ways: They either deny the child's fear—"Oh, come on, there's nothing to be afraid of. What's wrong with you anyway?"—or they overprotect— "Come into bed with me, honey, then you won't feel afraid." It seems to me that these responses are adaptive in the natural order and serve an important purpose in the animal kingdom.

Think of the baby bird, ready to take flight. It stands on the edge of its nest and looks down. It feels a moment of instinctual fear at the drop upon which its looking. This fear has kept it from wandering out of the nest before it was ready to fly. But mother bird knows the time is right, that there is nothing to fear, and so denies the baby's fear by pushing it out of the nest. Out of a sheer survival instinct, baby bird opens its wings and discovers that Mother bird was right, there was no need to fear.

On the other hand, perhaps a hawk is circling, looking for a tasty baby bird morsel for lunch. Baby bird is frightened, so is mother bird—there is danger present. Mother bird goes into protection mode, perhaps trying to lure the hawk away by pretending she has a broken wing or perhaps attacking the hawk outright. She doesn't expect baby bird to defend itself. To ensure its survival, she acts protectively, even aggressively.

For human beings, however, fear is not so cut and dried. We have the ability to think in the abstract, to worry beyond any present danger. Thus, we fear the unknown and the imaginary. We fear feelings, relationships, confrontation. We fear things that haven't happened and may never happen. Baby bird feels the present danger of falling from its nest, or the present danger of the hawk circling, but it doesn't sit in its nest worrying about the possibility of nuclear war or the dark. Baby bird is only afraid of things that are present—fire is to be feared only if the nest, tree, or forest is actually on fire. It doesn't worry about the possibilities "Will the tree catch fire tomorrow? What if someone climbs up the tree and sets it on fire while mommy bird is away?" For human beings, the issue of fear is much more complex than it is for animals, and either denying our children's fear or protecting our children when they're afraid isn't necessarily going to be helpful. Thus our response to our children's fear must be measured, weighed, and carefully thought out.

Developmental Stages

One thing to consider when your child exhibits fear is whether it is appropriate to his particular developmental stage. I'm always hesitant to write about developmental stages, because sometimes parents take it as license to sit back and do nothing; "It's a stage, it'll pass" is a common enough phrase for some parents. But inaction when your child is afraid is always inappropriate. I think looking at how fear manifests itself at different ages during the elementary school years is helpful, because it can ease your mind when the action you take doesn't work. Conversely, if your child is suddenly exhibiting an abnormal amount of fear for her age, it can be a signal to pay attention, perhaps something deeper is going on.

According to Frances L. Ilg, Louise Bates Ames, and Sidney M. Baker, in their book *Child Behavior*, children develop fears in a fairly predicable, patterned manner. Likewise, fears fade in a fairly predictable way as well. Let's look at a brief overview of the ages at which fear is likely to manifest itself.

In general, five-year-olds have relatively few fears. This is a concrete and fairly stable age. If five-year-olds are afraid, they will be afraid of concrete things such as falling down and hurting themselves.

Ages six and seven, on the other hand, are usually very fearful ages. A new stage of development, which permits the child to think more abstractly, has taken place. Thus, six- and seven-year-olds are likely to be afraid of something that might happen to them or to their mother or father. They may be afraid of being robbed or poisoned. They may become preoccupied with what to do if there's a fire, flood, or earthquake. These are ages where there may be a recurrence of separation anxiety, because a child fears Mom or Dad will die when he is at school. Many six- and seven-year-olds worry excessively about nuclear war, asteroids hitting the earth, and other concepts they may have been introduced to via the media.

Eight- and nine-year-olds, in contrast, generally have less fear. They may take their responsibilities more seriously and fear failure, but they are less likely to worry unreasonably. It should be noted, however, that eight-year-olds in particular may be very possessive about Mom's attention, almost as if they cannot get enough of her. One mother described it by saying "He's all over me! He wants to sit in my lap, to be with me all the time, to have my exclusive attention. It's like he could just crawl back into my womb!" This possessiveness may be interpreted by some parents as "clingy" or seen as another form of separation anxiety and thus be labeled "fearful." Be careful not to misinterpret your eight-year-old's behavior in this way; in general, it is simply a natural part of the developmental process for this age.

In general, ten is a relatively fearful age. Like six- and seven-year-olds, ten-year-olds may be afraid of things that they have heard about but that haven't actually happened to them. At ten the children also are beginning to differentiate between what they are afraid of and what they are not afraid of. This may result in some striking contrasts. For example, a child may be afraid of murderers and burglars on the one hand but not be afraid of being left by herself in the house.

Handling Fear

How we communicate with our children when they are afraid requires that we delicately balance stimulating their independence with acknowledging their fear.

"My daughter, who is seven and a half, is suddenly having a lot of difficulty right around bedtime. She's filled with questions like 'Mommy, what if when you're asleep, a burglar comes in and you don't know it because he sneaks past your room? What if he comes into my room and poisons me while I'm sleeping and I never see you again?' I know she's afraid, and I don't want her to repress her feelings, so I always say 'It sounds like you're afraid,' and 'Everyone feels afraid sometimes,' and things like that. But it goes on and on and on! She gets more elaborate, and sometimes she even begins to cry and cling to me and say 'I don't want to die.' I keep reflecting feelings, but it just doesn't go away. And the other night, she came into our bedroom, hysterical, and she said she wanted to sleep with us because she was afraid. Her father said, 'She's only a kid, let her sleep with us if she's afraid.' And then he turned to her and said, 'Don't worry, honey, we'll protect you. You'll be safe with us.' I know that he meant well, but since then it's been even worse."

These parents are making the common mistake of overindulging their daughter's fear. In doing so, they are overprotecting her. When Dad said "We'll protect you" and invited their daughter into bed with them, he inadvertently sent the message to his daughter that there may indeed be something to fear. In addition, he may have given his daughter the impression that she wasn't capable of handling nighttime on her own. These messages tear away at a child's confidence and ultimately result in lowered self-esteem.

Overt Messages vs. Covert Messages

We've talked about the differences between what parents say and what children hear them say in Chapter 2. Let's look at some common phrases that parents may use when their child is afraid and see how they probably come across to the child.

What the Parent Says	What the Child Thinks:
(Negatively Perceived Statements):	
"There's nothing to be afraid of."	"My feelings are wrong."
"Don't be afraid."	"I'm not allowed to feel this way."
"I'll protect you."	"There must be something to protect me from."
"You'll be safe with me."	"I won't be safe without you."

(Positively Perceived
Statements):

"Seems like you're feeling a little scared."	"Mom/Dad understands how I feel."
"Everyone feels afraid sometimes."	"I'm normal."
"This house is safe."	"I'm safe in this house."
"Can you think of something that will help you feel less afraid?"	"Mom/Dad has confidence in my abilities. She/he thinks I can handle this."

Putting It Together—Acknowledging Feelings

Let's see how parents can take the positively perceived messages just listed and use them in a real-life situation. Remember the parent at the beginning of this chapter whose daughter became afraid in their suddenly bigger house? Let's see how that mother used positively perceived messages to stimulate her daughter's independence and help the girl handle her own fear.

"I decided to sit down and speak with my daughter about her fear during the day, when her feelings were less intense. I began by saying 'I've noticed that you've been feeling a little apprehensive lately when I'm in a different room from you.' Immediately her eyes widened, and she said, 'I'm scared. I don't want to be by myself.' I said, 'Seems like it's a little more difficult now that the house is bigger,' and she nodded 'yes.' I went on and acknowledged her feelings a couple more times. I used words like 'concerned,' 'overwhelmed,' and 'unsure.' Then I told her that I wanted her to know that this house was safe, and I asked her what she thought she might be able to do to feel safe now that it was bigger. She just shook her head and said there was nothing to do."

So far, this mother is doing a great job. She begins by acknowledging her daughter's feelings, and rather than using the more intense feeling words like "scared," and "afraid," she reframes the fear in subtler words that have a less powerful feeling to them. This will help her child in the long run because it's easier to handle feeling "concerned" than it is to handle feeling "terrified."

Your Child's Script

Remember as you work through this communication process with your child that it is a script. The benefit of following a script that many other parents have used successfully with their children is that you can be relatively sure that the process will have similar results when you use it with your children. That's not to say that we're all "wired" in the same way, or that we're robots or computers that can be preprogrammed. We are, however, all human beings, and good communication techniques do affect us all in a similar fashion.

Just as you follow a script, your child has a script as well. In general, that script is a negative one. In other words, it's comprised of one word: *"No!"*

There are, of course, variations on this theme: "There's nothing to do," "I can't think of anything," "Nothing will help," being a few of them. As I've said before, try not to be discouraged by your child's negativity. Remember that it's simply a script and that in spite of their negative attitude, this process still seems to produce positive results.

Stimulating Independence

Once you've acknowledged your child's fear, it's time to stimulate her independence. Without this step, you may inadvertently overindulge the fear or convey to your child that there is something to be afraid of when there's not.

"After my daughter said that there was nothing she could think of to help her feel safe, I decided to offer some suggestions that I had thought of before I engaged her in this conversation. So I said, 'What do you think would happen if we found a way that you could communicate with me even if we were in different parts of the house?' I guess this piqued her curiosity, because instead of just being negative, she said, 'Like what?' So I said, 'Well, what do you think would happen if we just started with nighttime, and we got a piece of string, and you could hold one end of it in bed, and I could hold the other, and if you needed to know where I was, you could tug on it, and I'd tug back?' 'I don't think that would work,' she said, 'because what if you had to walk around?' So I said, 'Well, what do you think would happen if we got some sort of intercom or walkie-talkie where we could talk to each other if we needed to?' I guess I knew that would appeal to her, and of course she said 'yes.' So the next day we bought walkie-talkies. The interesting thing was that we used them for maybe a week very regularly. The next week I would sometimes find her walkie-talkie lying on a table, and she'd be off doing something in another room. And then she just dropped it all together. She still uses the walkie-talkies to play with friends when they come over, but it's like they gave her her confidence back."

Here again, Mom did a good job. Rather than trying to think up solutions on the spot in her conversation with her daughter, she took time beforehand to think not only about what alternatives would be acceptable to her but which ones might appeal to her daughter as well. Notice, too, that Mom phrased her suggestions as questions. Doing this has two benefits: (1) It gives ownership of the decision to the daughter and makes it more likely that she will internalize and stick with the solution as time goes on; and (2) It doesn't block communication, which might result in an escalation of the fear behavior.

Remember, too, that while this mother and daughter chose a

"high-tech" solution with the walkie-talkies, if you can't afford something like that, or if you simply find it unappealing, you wouldn't offer it as a solution. Many parents with this same sort of problem have successfully offered solutions (for nighttime fears) such as glow-in-the-dark stars stuck on the ceiling of the bedroom, a flashlight, a night-light, or a "Morse code" where the child can knock on the floor, ceiling, or wall and have the parent knock back. And even though the suggestion of tugging on a string didn't work for the mother and daughter in this story, it has been successful for others. For daytime fears, other parents have offered solutions such as letting the child carry around an item belonging to the parent or making up a "contract" that spells out to the child that the parent won't leave the house without telling her. Whatever solution you ultimately offer, keep in mind to phrase it as a question, and leave it up to the child to choose something that will best help her.

Setting Limits to Stimulate Independence

"My eight-year-old and I went through this, and he chose to have a flashlight at night. But it ultimately didn't work. After I got him the flashlight he still wanted me to be by his side until he fell asleep."

The final step in stimulating your child's independence lies in setting limits. Because limits give children a feeling of safety and security in their environment and convey to them a feeling that you as the parent know what you're doing, they build confidence and self-esteem and instill courage in children. We set limits by giving "I" messages and offering choices with consequences. When the father in this last scenario was given these tools, here's what happened:

"I sat down with my son and told him that going to sleep by himself was something he could do. He started to protest and say he

was afraid, that he needed me to stay with him until he fell asleep. I told him that I knew he felt a little nervous at night, and I also knew that this was something he could do. I told him that beginning that night, I wasn't going to stay, and if he could think of anything besides the flashlight that would help, I'd be happy to try and work with him on a solution. That night, when he got in bed, he began to protest again. So I said, 'When you delay bedtime, I feel frustrated, because this is time I need to do other things. I would like you to close your eyes and go to sleep.' He begged me to stay just one more minute, and I said, 'Either close your eyes and try to sleep, or I'll think the light from the door being open is keeping you awake, and I'll close the door. You decide.' I couldn't believe it, but it worked! My son stayed in bed and over the next couple of weeks the fear dissipated."

When Dad set a limit on his son's behavior, he conveyed the message that he believed in his son. I truly believe that most children work toward "wholeness" and want to feel a sense of accomplishment in their lives. Fear is not necessarily a pleasant emotion, and most children really would rather not feel afraid. Thus when you combine an understanding of how a child feels with firm limits and confidence that they can handle it, you free them to be courageous.

The Child Who Continues to Test You

"My concern is that if I told my child that I'd close the door as a consequence, he'd simply get out of bed, open the door, and maybe even come into the living room."

Although I wouldn't point it out to the child, a fearful child is not one who's likely to get out of bed when you leave. Should it happen, though, you might want to think of a consequence that you have control over. Perhaps you could say "Either get back in bed, or tomorrow night you can go to bed when it's still light outside so you won't be afraid. You decide."

Building Courage Systematically

I recommend a daily exercise to parents as a way of building and maintaining high self-esteem and courage in their children. It involves writing a note to your child on a daily basis, and putting it in your child's lunch box or backpack for him to discover and read at school. (Children who don't read yet are invariably curious about the note and often will ask the teacher to read it for them.) Whether your child reads yet or not, this exercise will systematically build courage in your child by giving him a little dose on a daily basis. Think of it as a courage vitamin. It should not be used instead of the techniques you've already learned, but in addition to them.

The Value of Lunch Box or Backpack Notes

Giving your child a note that she can read during the day when you're not there has a number of benefits. First of all, it will give her the feeling that you've touched base with her in the middle of the day even though you're not physically present at school. The internal resources that your child begins the day with can be diminished by lunchtime. Your note will help replenish those resources and get her through the rest of the day. In addition, the written word is powerful. Many people believe what they read, but if they were to hear someone express the same thing verbally, they would discount it. Children, too, believe the written word. Writing to your children to build their courage not only ensures that they take it seriously, but makes them less likely to discount your compliments because they're trying to "save face" or "be cool." In addition, when you build your child's courage in writing, it gives the child the opportunity to receive it at his own pace and look at it again whenever he might need a pick-me-up.

One mother's nine-year-old son was extremely fearful at school, clinging to the teacher day after day, making every choice dependent on the teacher's approval or advice. His mother began writing daily lunch box notes to him. The first day when he got home from school, he said in a rough voice, "Hey, what was that dumb note in my lunch box anyway?" She simply said, "I just felt like writing you a note." The next day, and for a week or so after that, he made no comment, but she kept writing the notes on a daily basis. One day she accidentally forgot the note. The next day, before he left for school, he asked, "Did you remember the note today?" Clearly, the notes had become important. Even more remarkable, however, was the change in his attitude at school. Less than three weeks after beginning the notes, the teacher pulled his mother aside and said, "I don't know what's happened to him, but all of a sudden, he's not dependent on me anymore. He doesn't cling, he makes decisions and moves around the room independently. He's simply not afraid anymore."

Content

As I mentioned previously, children should receive a lunch box/backpack note from their parents daily, even on the weekends and during the summer. Rather than being placed in a lunch box on non–school days, a note can just as easily be pinned to a child's pillow or placed underneath the breakfast plate to find.

In order to have these notes work toward building courage and self-esteem, I suggest that they have a very specific content. I recommend that you alternate between expressing unconditional love one day and either expressing concrete positive expectations or observing a past positive event the next day.

The Three Note Types

Notes that express unconditional love essentially tell your child that she doesn't need to do anything or be anything other than what she is in order for you to love her. Your "I love you" in this type of note should not be tied in to any behavior your child has exhibited. For example, do *not* say "I love you when you do your homework on time," because this implies that you don't love him when his homework is not done on time.

Notes that express concrete positive expectations send the message to your child that you have confidence in her abilities and that you believe in her.

Notes that talk about positive observable events tell your child that you're paying attention and that you've noticed some positive thing he did.

Let me give you an example to show you what I mean.

Day 1 *(Unconditional love):* "Dear _____, You are a terrific kid, and Daddy (Mommy) and I love you just because you're you."

Day 2 *(Concrete positive expectations):* "Dear _____, I know you've been worried about your spelling test today. I've noticed how hard you've been working at memorizing the words, and I know it will serve you well. I'll be thinking about you."

Day 3 *(Unconditional love):* "Dear _____, I love you even when we differ. I love growing with you."

Day 4 *(Observation of a past positive event):* "Dear _____, I noticed that you cleared your plate from the table last night without even being asked. Thanks for acting so responsibly."

And so on . . .

When used in this structured way, lunch box or backpack notes are a simple yet extremely powerful way to communicate with and build the self-esteem of your children. I urge you to keep in mind that you may not get an immediate response to your notes, and you should resist the temptation to ask about them. Remember that if you ask your child if she took her vitamin day after day, eventually she may resist taking it. Instead of asking, rest assured that when you use these notes on a daily basis, you eventually will *see* the results—they work miracles, bond relationships, eliminate fears, and instill values and morals.

When Intervention by a Professional Is Required

A chapter on the fearful child wouldn't be complete without a word of caution. There are times when parental intervention simply isn't enough and the advice and/or therapeutic intervention of a trained professional is necessary. To determine if your child needs professional intervention, use the following guidelines:

1. Has your child experienced a trauma recently? At the beginning of the chapter, I mentioned a child whose friend was killed crossing the street. This is a situation that requires professional intervention. That's not to say that as the parent, you can't write lunch box notes, or express empathy, or set limits, but it's important to understand that your intervention probably will have only limited success.

2. Is the fear disproportionate to your child's developmental level? Does she appear unduly afraid of something that she might have limited or no knowledge of? For example, is she suddenly afraid of being raped? Because fear can signal that something happened to your child that you don't know about, it would be important to get a professional's opinion just to make sure.

3. In addition to the fear, is your child exhibiting any other unusual behavior, such as self-mutilation, excessive and inappropriate masturbation, use of language that hasn't been introduced in your own household, inappropriate or unusually aggressive play with toys or other children? Has your child's appetite suddenly changed? Is he eating in excess or suddenly starving himself? Has his schoolwork suddenly deteriorated? Does he appear suddenly to be afraid of a particular situation or person yet unafraid the rest of the time? If you answered "yes" to any one of these questions, I would highly recommend that you take your child to a professional who can help determine if he simply is going through a normal developmental stage or if something traumatic has happened to him.

Chapter 10
When Parents Disagree

Your Child and Your Partner

At any given workshop or lecture, I have a mixture of men and women. Sometimes couples will attend together, other times I'll have only one parent in a two-parent household present, and always I have a good sprinkling of single parents mixed in. Invariably, as I begin talking about the techniques, a man or woman who is attending without a partner will ask, "How important is it that my partner and I do this the same way? And what do you do if your values and ideas about child rearing are different than those of your partner?"

Disagreement between parents is a natural part of child rearing. In fact, given our different backgrounds, upbringings, and personalities, it's hard to see why parents would ever agree! But the truth is that when parents don't agree about disciplining or communicating with the children, and especially when they disagree in front of the children, it can become problematic to the point of actually contributing to the children's misbehavior.

Acting as a Team

Think for a moment about how it would be to run a business if your business partner disagreed with you every step of the way. Imagine a staff meeting where your employees are gathered around the table along with you and your business partner. Your partner makes a remark, and you vehemently disagree with him. He argues his point, you argue yours, but no real resolution is reached. You drop the matter and move on, rolling your eyes as you do so. Now he brings up a suggestion to improve productivity. You put him down, claiming it's a "stupid idea." He gets angry and storms out. Consider what your employees would think of this situation. Would they feel comfortable or uncomfortable? Do you think they'd believe their jobs are secure? Do you think they would be able to continue to fulfill their responsibilities within this kind of business partnership and management style?

In a family, just as in a business, a lack of teamwork between the leaders creates difficulties for the group as a whole. When children perceive that Mom and Dad aren't acting as a team, they get the feeling that their parents don't really know what they're doing. In this situation most children feel unprotected and unsafe and wonder about the security of their family—just as employees would wonder about job security. The children's unspoken thought is that "If Mom and Dad aren't in agreement, who's in charge? If no one is in charge, then how safe is this situation?" Children whose parents argue a lot may be prone to sleep disturbances, separation difficulties, and undue anxiety because they feel unsafe. One of the most important things we can do for our children when living in a two-parent household is to work together on raising the children and act as a team.

The Creation of a Power Gap

Living in a family in which the parents fail to operate as a team essentially creates a power gap. When children perceive that a gap exists in power, they will take advantage of the fighting and "fill the power gap." They may do this through manipulation, tantrums, physical aggression, whining, tears, rudeness, excessive pleading, or explosive outbursts. All of these things serve children in getting their way or in receiving negative attention from their parents. How powerful the children feel when a simple tantrum can get parents in a frenzy, or when a mere manipulative trick can win them something that they originally were told they couldn't have! The irony is that even though children may feel more powerful, they also know on some level that it's inappropriate for them to wield this kind of power and it doesn't quite feel comfortable. They may, therefore, create conflict in hopes of getting Mom and Dad to take the power back.

Out of the Chaos

Children live in a challenging, many times chaotic world. From birth, their brains are busy trying to organize the information they are receiving and make sense of it. For this to happen successfully, it helps if they are presented with a somewhat calm, organized world at home. As parents, it's our job to refrain from contributing to the chaos with undue fighting. That's not to say that children should never see Mom and Dad fight. In order for children to learn how to resolve conflicts, they must be exposed to conflict resolution. Likewise, for children to learn how healthy families and relationships work, they must be exposed to parents who communicate respectfully, who place primary importance on the spousal bond, and who refrain from undermining each other's authority. Mom and Dad must communicate the message to the children that they are in charge and they feel comfortable being in charge.

In order to more fully understand and ultimately resolve your parenting conflicts with your partner, it might be helpful to discuss what your beliefs are and what "style" of parenting you'd like to have in your family.

Parenting Style

Prior to having children, I'm willing to bet you never sat down with each other and discussed how you were parented or what you considered your "parenting style" to be. In all likelihood, you were caught up in the romance of the relationship and figured that agreement on how to raise your children would come naturally. If you're like most parents, however, what you soon discovered after the kids arrived is that many times your ideas about what to do in a particular situation are strikingly different than those of your partner. But even if you haven't discussed it before, it is never too late to discuss how to parent. Try sitting down with your partner, considering the following information, and answering the questions that follow.

Autocratic Parenting

An autocratic style of parenting is piloted by the belief that "Because you live under my roof, you have to do what I say. The rules are nonnegotiable, I make them up, I don't have to explain them to you, and that's that. When you're eighteen, you can do what you want, but I'm the king (queen) of this castle and you must obey me." Autocratic parents often believe that their primary responsibility is to protect their children.

Permissive Parenting

At the heart of a permissive style of parenting is the belief that you don't need to set limits or have rules for your children. Permissive parents believe that "If I give my children enough rope, they'll hang themselves. Society will provide the limits my children need. I don't need to be involved, I can be their friend." Permissive parents often believe that their primary responsibility is to be their children's friend and allow their children to experience life on their own.

Authoritative, Democratic, or Cooperative Parenting

An authoritative, democratic, or cooperative style of parenting takes into account the ideas of individual family members and recognizes and respects the individual members' temperament and developmental level. Parents who subscribe to these parenting styles believe their job in the family is not only to protect their children but to prepare them to be independent, ethical adults someday. The parent holds the belief that "I am in charge, and I feel comfortable being in charge. I can allow my children to voice their opinions about my rules because I am comfortable with my role as leader in the family. When my child has a good suggestion for changing our limits, I can compromise without feeling my authority is being undermined. I also am willing to stand firm in the face of tears, threats, anger, and hysteria if I believe that a rule is nonnegotiable." These parents often believe that fostering cooperation and open communication are keys to a healthy family.

Conversing with Your Partner About Style

In order for you and your partner to become a team, each of you should consider and discuss the following questions.

Your History

- How were you parented? What style did your father subscribe to? How about your mother? When you were a child, how did you feel about the way you were parented? Did it make you want to cooperate? Rebel? Give up? Ignore your parents? Leave home?

- How do you think the way you were parented influences the way you parent now?
- Are there aspects of your parents' style(s) that you dislike seeing in yourself?
- Are there ways in which you were parented that you'd like to emulate?
- Are there similarities between your answers and those of your partner? Where do you differ?

Your Goals as a Parent

Keeping in mind the way each of you were parented and how you felt about your parents' style(s) both as a child and now as an adult, think about what goals you'd like to create together in developing a philosophy for raising your children.

- What traits or qualities would you like your children to have as adults?
- How do you see your role in the family?
- What is your child's role?
- What responsibilities do you think parents have in raising their children?
- What responsibilities should children have as part of the family unit?
- What style of parenting seems to best fit your goals?

This kind of in-depth questioning often brings parents closer together in their child-rearing philosophies. While it doesn't always bring agreement on every issue, this discussion can help you recognize why your partner might have strong feelings about certain rules or limits.

"My wife and I used to disagree about almost every aspect of raising our children. I thought she was too 'soft' and she was always talking about their feelings. She thought I was harsh and way too strict, and that I never took into consideration what opinion the kids had about something. We made a date to sit down and talk through our parenting backgrounds and to make up a list of goals for parenting our kids. I have to say, I was really surprised at how much we didn't know about each other, even after eleven years of marriage. I had no idea that her father was such a strict disciplinarian and that she never felt heard by him or close to him when she was growing up. I realized that she might be a little soft with our kids because she was really reacting against how her father had treated her. I had a strict upbringing too, but I always felt my parents were fair. So I just wanted to raise our kids the way I had been raised. When we put down our goals for how we wanted our kids to turn out as adults, we realized that we both actually wanted the same things for them—that they be sensitive and loving, that they be responsible and kind, that they cooperate around the house and with others. I guess during that talk, we both realized that it was important to balance discipline with talking about feelings. I still think my wife is a little too easy on the kids, but instead of fighting about it with her in the moment, I know where she's coming from, and I bring it up with her later. We usually can have a rational conversation at that point and reach a compromise for the next time."

Recognizing the history behind each other's perspective helped this couple honor and respect each other so that they could back each other up in front of the children without feeling threatened themselves.

Chapter 11
Soothing Sibling Rivalry

Children and Siblings

When my daughter was seven and a half and her little brother was just past two, he nicknamed her "Mimi," not yet being able to quite get his mouth around the three syllables of her name: Emilie. One day he toddled up to me and began "Mommy says . . ." and then his voice trailed off. I replied, "What does Mommy say?" He looked earnestly at me and said again, "Mommy says . . ." Again I repeated, "What does Mommy say?" He looked contemplative for a moment, then he said, "Daddy says . . ." I smiled and decided I was along for the ride, so I good-naturedly asked, "What does Daddy say?" He furrowed his brow, concentrating, and said, "Daddy says . . ." Again I asked, "What does Daddy say?" Now he decided to bring his sister into the conversation and said, "Mimi says . . ." So I said, "What does Mimi say?" To which he replied, "Mimi says *'Don't touch that toy!'* "

I think this story about my children illustrates what the sibling relationship is all about. While my son couldn't think of what anyone else in the family might say in their relationship to him, he had no doubt in his mind about the nature of his relationship with his sister. And that relationship—the sibling relationship—is unique among all the other relationships that our children ever will have in their lives. It can be fiercely competitive, close and loving, or distant and cold. As parents, we have a choice. We can facilitate the relationship, or we can interfere with the course of its natural development.

Sibling Rivalry

"My twenty-month-old daughter started to cry and when I went in, there was my five-year-old son standing there. She had a red welt on her forehead and I was convinced he'd hit her, but he denied it. I began interrogating him and wound up accusing him of hitting her. I found out later that she'd hit her head going under a table. I felt so guilty!"

"I walked into my infant son's room where he was lying in his playpen. My six-year-old son had taken every item of clothing out of the dresser drawers and piled it on top of my four-month-old. I was horrified!"

Siblings. They find ingenious ways of getting parents' attention and of torturing each other. Likewise, parents of more than one child tend to be on the alert for "sibling rivalry." And especially alert when that rivalry takes the form of physical violence. How we handle conflict, or our suspicion of conflict between our children is of critical importance. Our expertise (or lack thereof) will determine how our children relate to one another, how they feel about themselves, and how we feel about them as well.

Not All Conflicts Are Created Equal

In order for you to handle sibling conflict in positive ways—that is, ways that enrich your children's relationship rather than ways that contribute to rivalry—it is important to recognize that not all conflicts are created equal. At first glance, the two situations I just related may seem similar. An older sibling is involved or is suspected of being involved in a conflict with a younger sibling. For the parents, it appeared in both cases that the older sibling had done something against the younger. In reality, however, the two situations are very different and require quite different handling on the part of the parent.

Assessing the Type of Conflict

The main, and perhaps most important, difference lies in what the parent knows about the situation rather than what the parent assumes. In both cases, the parent did not see one child doing anything to the other. In essence, the parent had walked in *after* the "crime" had been committed. However, in the first scenario, the parent drew conclusions about what had happened based on her assumptions. In the past, her son had hit her daughter. Seeing them standing close together, a red welt on the younger one's forehead, she assumed that her son had once again resorted to hitting. In the second scenario, while the parent hadn't actually *seen* the older child take the clothing out of the drawers, it's unlikely that they jumped out by themselves. Likewise, the four-month-old was too young to be involved. The parent in the second situation could easily *and correctly* draw the conclusion that the older had placed the clothes on top of the younger based on the facts in front of her.

The first step in handling sibling conflict is to separate situations based on the facts. There are four basic possibilities:

1. You're in the room and observe the conflict, so you know exactly what happened, but you believe your children are old enough to work it out themselves. ("Old enough" would be children who are verbal, usually age three or four and above.)

2. You're not in the room, so you didn't see what happened. You're pretty sure you know, but you would have to rely on past experiences and/or assumptions to make a guess.
3. You're in the room and observe the conflict, so you know exactly what happened, but your children are either too young (not verbal) to handle it themselves and/or the situation was dangerous and warrants intervention from you as the leader in the family.
4. You're not in the room, so you didn't see what happened, but you can make a correct guess that doesn't involve *any* assumptions on your part.

These four possibilities can be divided into two groups that will facilitate your handling of the situation and preserve your children's relationship as well as their self-esteem.

When you believe that your children can work an argument out themselves or if you weren't in the room and don't really know what happened (numbers 1 and 2 above), you'll want to practice late or nonintervention.

The Benefits of Late or Nonintervention

The benefits of late or nonintervention when siblings are in conflict are similar to those achieved when you refrain from intervening in peer conflict. One main difference, however, is that this wait-and-see attitude also helps you avoid labeling one child as the perpetrator of all conflict. Many parents have a tendency to take sides, usually coming down harder on the older child, believing that he or she "should know better." This creates a situation where one child is seen as the victim, the other as the bully. Soon they will act out these assigned roles, especially since there are advantages for each. Victims usually get quite a bit of attention; thus a child who has been assigned that role is likely to set things up so that she's consistently seen in this light. She may "nudge" her brother, "poke at" her sister, whine or follow a sibling around until the sibling is provoked into action. The child who has been assigned the role of bully usually feels as if he's always "wrong" and can't do anything right. Operating from this base of lowered self-esteem, he soon begins to live up to his parents' expectations. The advantage for the bully is that he doesn't have to struggle with problem solving. Since he's expected to be aggressive, he'll resort to that rather than looking for alternative solutions to being "nudged," "poked," or "whined at" by a sibling.

When practicing late or nonintervention, remember to ask yourself if the children really need your help. The rule of thumb here, as in peer conflict, is whether a child is being hurt or whether a child has asked for your help. If you must intervene, it's extremely important that you keep your voice as calm and even as possible, remembering that you're not there to judge but to assist your children in solving *their* problem. Remember, too, that when your children are out of control, what they need most is a parent who is in control. Likewise, the less you judge, the more likely your children are to develop a positive sibling relationship, and the more "fair" you will appear to be.

Intervention

When you are called on to intervene in your children's problem, the first statement you will address to your children is: "Seems like there's a problem here." This may be met with a variety of responses. Usually the children will turn to you to arbitrate, attempting to convince you that each of them is in the right and that the other should be punished. Their voices are likely to escalate, and momentary chaos may ensue. Don't get caught up in this. Your job is to *facilitate* problem solving, *not* solve the problem. If you try to solve the problem, you will end up being the judge and jury, one child will inevitably feel "blamed," and you won't have given your children's relationship the opportunity to develop in a positive way. Stay calm and recognize *both* children's feelings.

You might say something like: "Seems like you're both really upset by this." When your children continue to squabble (notice I said "when," not "if"), you might add a few more statements that would acknowledge their feelings, such as: "Megan, you seem really angry, and John seems defensive. What seems to be the problem?" Should both children (or all the children, depending on how many you have) talk at the same time, you can add, "I can't really hear when both of you are talking. Who would like to go first?" By asking the children who should go first, you will avoid seeming to take sides by naming one or the other.

Remember Your Listening Skills

As the story begins to unfold, listen with your body as well as your ears. Pay attention by making eye contact with the speaker, keep your body turned toward the children, and don't engage in another activity while you're listening. Acknowledge that you hear what's being said by giving verbal cues such as "Uh-huh" and "I see." Be empathetic by acknowledging the feelings being expressed. Say things like "Sounds like that made you angry" and "Seems like you felt really pushed around when that happened." If the other child tries to interrupt, calmly state that he'll have a turn in a minute. Say that you feel both sides are too important to miss hearing, and that's why you've asked them to take turns.

Restating What You Hear

As you listen, restate what you hear. For example: "Megan, it sounds like you're suggesting that John shouldn't touch your things without asking you first," or "John, I hear you saying that you didn't mean to break Megan's toy, it was an accident." Be careful that you restate only what was said without interjecting an opinion of your own. For example, *don't say:* "So, Megan, Johnny always touches your things without asking," or "John broke your toy by accident, Megan, he didn't mean to." By phrasing your "restatements" beginning with the words "It sounds like . . ." and "I hear you saying . . ." you will avoid taking sides. There's nothing more frustrating when you're trying to help than to be dragged into the argument when one child accuses you of siding with the other.

Support a Solution

When you've heard the story from both (or all) sides, support the children in arriving at a solution. To do this, ask the question: "What do you two think should be done about this?" Your children may be surprised. In the past, it is likely that you tried to arbitrate, and they won't be expecting to have the responsibility turned over to them. As they begin to sort through different solutions (which they probably won't do calmly at first; in fact, it is likely that their argumentative attitudes and loud voices actually will increase), be patient. Use the restatement technique again, saying things such as "So, Megan, I hear you saying that you'd feel better if John asked before going into your room," and "John, you seem unhappy with that solution, what would you suggest?" By working through suggestions calmly, restating what you hear, and watching your children's faces for their reactions to the solutions presented, it's likely that you'll be able to facilitate the problem-solving process.

Achieving Conclusion

If it seems as if your children are getting nowhere or that the process is taking an unreasonable length of time, you should make a summary statement, then leave the decision for what the solution will be in the hands of your children. It might sound something like this: "This sounds like a tough problem. You're doing a great job discussing it, and I know you'll think of something. If I can help, come get me, I'll be in the other room reading the newspaper." Many times children will come up with a solution quickly at this point. Even if they don't, your encouraging words will give them the confidence they need to solve their own problems.

When Discipline Is Called For

"The other day I was in the room with my nine-year-old son and seven-year-old daughter. They were having a verbal argument about something, and all of a sudden my daughter reached over and slapped my son's face. I was shocked."

When one of our children deliberately hurts the other—whether they're in our presence or not—it is shocking. Yet even in the most loving of households, this may happen. Children don't necessarily have the impulse control that allows for rational thought in the midst of intense feelings. Thus there will be times when physical outbursts may occur. At these times, it may be necessary to take a firmer tack that has limit setting at its roots. Let's review the situations described at the beginning of this chapter that would require that you discipline one or more of the children.

1. You're in the room and observe the conflict, so you know what happened, but your children are too young (not verbal) to handle it themselves or the situation was dangerous or potentially dangerous and requires setting a limit. This is the situation described by the man with the seven- and nine-year old children. Although his children were verbal, the situation involved bodily harm that he observed.
2. You're not in the room, so you didn't see what happened, but someone got hurt, and you can make a guess about what happened that doesn't involve *any* assumptions on your part. This is the case described in

the beginning of the chapter, where the six-year-old took all the clothes out of the drawers and piled them on top of the four-month-old.

Ensure Safety

Obviously, when danger is involved and discipline is called for, the first step will be to remove the child(ren) from the danger, either by separating them or by removing a dangerous object. Sometimes this separation automatically will result in a cooling-down period for one or both children in their own room or space. It's valuable to understand that just because discipline is called for, it needn't be immediate to be effective. There's no reason you can't discipline a child who's hurt her sibling after she's cooled off.

Don't Ask Questions You Already Know the Answer To

One of my favorite cartoons shows a little girl playing with Scotch tape. As the cartoon progresses, the child gets more and more covered with the tape. Her mother walks in and says, looking at her, "Have you been playing with my Scotch tape again?" The little girl looks up at her mother and thinks, "Gee, if she doesn't know, *I'm* sure not going to tell her!"

While it's tempting to walk into a sibling conflict and try to extract a confession from the guilty party, most of the time it only makes the child dig herself in more deeply. Asking children questions to which we already know the answer sets them up to lie. Then you not only have a child who has injured a sibling but one who is trying to save face as well. Instead of asking your child if she hit her brother, or if he piled the clothes on top of the four-month-old, state it as fact: "I feel shocked that you hit your brother," or "I see you piled the clothes on top of your brother." This way you can deal with the misbehavior instead of having to handle the side issue of lying as well.

A Typical Situation

"My seven- and nine-year-old daughters were sitting at the coffee table doing their homework. I was in the bathroom with my three-year-old son and I could hear my oldest daughter, Jennifer, humming to herself as she worked. Then I heard my younger one, Katherine, ask her a question. Jennifer just kept humming. I heard Katherine repeat herself a couple of times, and each time Jennifer just kept humming. I was still helping my son when Jennifer came into the bathroom. Her eyes were filled with tears, and she turned on the water and began washing what looked like a small black spot on her hand. When I asked her what happened, she said Katherine had poked a pencil into her hand. I was so furious that literally 'saw red.' I sent Jennifer back into the room and told her I'd be there in a minute. Though I didn't say so to Jennifer, I needed a moment to catch my breath and think. I guess one thing I've learned about siblings is that there's rarely such a thing as only one person fighting. I knew that Jennifer couldn't be blameless, but because I wasn't there, I didn't know exactly what happened."

Mom did a good job here. Rather than flying into the room in a rage, she knew that both her daughters were out of immediate danger, and she took a moment to get herself together. She also correctly assessed that she didn't have all the facts and that it was likely that the poking had not been unprovoked. Because injury was incurred, discipline is called for. The next step for Mom will be to give an abbreviated "I" message to both of the girls.

The Abbreviated "I" Message

An abbreviated "I" message works in much the same way as the "I" message I described in Chapter 8. The difference is that you'll delay the ending of the "I" message so that feelings can be acknowledged.

"I walked back into the room, and I was very stern. I looked both girls in the eyes and said, 'When you girls get into physical fights, I feel shocked and angry and extremely disappointed because you know that there are other ways to solve problems.' They looked at me wordlessly. Then I said, 'What happened here?' I listened to both sides of the story, and by putting it together I think I figured out approximately what happened. Apparently, Katherine was annoyed that Jennifer wasn't responding to her, so she took Jennifer's pencil. Jennifer tried to grab it back, and they pulled back and forth for a minute before Jennifer let go. Because they were tugging with such force, the eraser end of the pencil hit Katherine in the face. That made her even more angry and she dug the point of the pencil into Jennifer's hand."

While it's not always necessary to "get the story" (for example, in the case of the six-year-old who buried his sibling under the clothes), in this case it proved helpful. Mom was able to piece together what she thought had happened and determine that both girls should be disciplined. Because she wasn't in the room, this is probably the safest course of action. However, there will be times when only one child requires disciplinary action. Make sure that if this is the case, you're absolutely certain that only one person was responsible; otherwise follow the problem-solving technique at the beginning of the chapter instead of setting limits.

Address Feelings and Act Empathetically

Now that Mom has established what happened and given an abbreviated "I" message, the next step should address feelings and provide empathy. This step helps sensitize the children to both their own and the other person's feelings.

"After I listened to the girls' explanations, I said, 'I'm hearing that Katherine was feeling ignored, and when she tried to get Jennifer's attention by taking the pencil away, Jennifer felt angry and disrupted. When you both tugged on the pencil, I guess you both started feeling angry, and because you didn't talk about your anger, you both got hurt.'"

This simple statement of feelings helps both girls feel understood by Mom, which will lessen them vying for her attention and sympathy. In addition, Mom did a great job when she resisted adding the word "but" as in "I guess you both started feeling angry *but* you should know that you aren't allowed to hurt each other." The word "but" negates the empathy both children need. The same thing holds true if only one child is responsible. Even though it's difficult to empathize with a child who has misbehaved, when we address our children's feelings of jealousy, anger, or sadness, it encourages them to understand the motivation behind their misbehavior. Identifying the roots of the aggression helps the child learn to express those natural feelings with words instead of aggressive acts. In hearing their sibling's feelings addressed, eventually they'll realize the impact that their actions have on others. In addition, if we discipline sibling rivalry without recognition of a child's motivation, one child usually winds up feeling "wronged"— and may assume that you're taking sides. This usually results in a repetition of the misbehavior. If you're having trouble with this part of the technique, remember that you don't need to *feel* empathy, just *act* empathetically.

Finishing the "I" Message and Giving a Consequence

"I told the girls that the next time they were feeling angry, I wanted them to express their feelings with words. Then I said, 'I feel so strongly that physical violence is unacceptable that I think you need a consequence for this.' At that point I felt a little at a loss, because I wasn't sure what a logical consequence would be. I didn't think separating them would help, because that would probably be more of a relief than anything else. So I decided to ask them for help. I said, 'What do you girls think the consequence should be?' "

Asking the Children to Help

Asking children for help in coming up with a consequence truly gives them responsibility for their own behavior. Many times children are far harsher than we would ever be. Remember as you do this that you'll be the final decision maker and you needn't accept any of the children's suggestions. Sometimes, though, hearing them talk can give you an idea of what would be appropriate.

"So Katherine's lip started to tremble, and Jennifer's eyes filled with tears. Finally Jennifer said in a small voice, 'I guess we could have no TV for the rest of the week.' I said, 'Well, that's one possibility,' even though I knew I wouldn't choose it because it wasn't logically related. Katherine said, 'No candy?' 'Another possibility,' I replied, 'but I'd really like to come up with something that's related to your fight. Since it didn't have anything to do with TV or candy, I'm not sure those are the best choices.' My daughter Jennifer said emotionally, 'It's hard to think of something,' and she put her hand to her heart. 'I just can't live with the guilt!' "

Giving the Consequence

"I managed to keep a straight face, and suddenly I had a thought about an appropriate consequence. I said, 'Well, here's what I think. I think that what I want is for both of you to understand what your feelings were before the fighting began. What led up to this. So here's the consequence. I want you to each write a paper and in it I want you to say what feelings you were having that made you upset enough to fight. Then I want you to write down what you could have done differently. Finally I want you to write an apology to each other.' With great seriousness, both girls got a sheet of paper out of their notebooks, and went to separate corners of the room to begin writing. It took them about twenty minutes, and I asked to see their papers before they showed them to each other. They'd both done a wonderful job, and I could tell that the apologies were heartfelt. In fact, I was especially touched to see at the end that each girl had written 'Can we still be friends?' It warmed my heart to think that they could feel not only like sisters but like friends as well."

Gender Differences?

"I would never be able to get my son to write a paper to his sister like that. I think boys are just different from girls."

I think boys are different from girls, too, in many, many significant ways. The way in which they're *not* different, however, is that they're still your children. As such, you have the right to impose any logical consequence you see fit and stick with it. If you feel that writing a paper is an appropriate consequence, whether your children are boys or girls, then be strict about enforcing that consequence.

There will be times when writing a paper, however, doesn't appeal to you for other reasons. Perhaps you feel it won't be effective, or maybe it doesn't logically fit the misbehavior. Sometimes choosing to separate the children is more logical, or taking something away (perhaps the object they were fighting about) will work more effectively. For any given situation, there are numerous consequences that can work toward diminishing sibling conflict.

Taking Away Your Attention as a Consequence

"My six-and-a-half-year-old son now knows enough not to actually hit his younger brother. But he threatens him. For example, he'll stand really close and murmur threatening things under his breath, and my younger son will burst into tears."

Sometimes consequences can be given more subtly than stating an either/or choice to your child. In this case, Dad could empathize with his younger son, reflecting his feelings of sadness or worry. Then Dad could ask if there was anything he could think of that would help. When his younger son doesn't come up with something, Dad could then ask, "Well, would it help if you and I went somewhere else and played for a while?" By focusing full attention on the victim, the older child will come to realize that there's no payoff for murmuring threatening things to his brother. Quite the opposite! When he murmurs threatening things, his brother gets a lot of attention from Daddy. This ought to be enough to stop the misbehavior. Don't forget, however, that the role of victim can be a seductive one. As I mentioned before, sometimes children who were authentically being victimized at the beginning will actively adopt this role when they realize that it receives a lot of attention. Watch your children's behavior carefully to ensure that this isn't taking place. One mother who used this technique too frequently reported that eventually when she went and picked up her younger son to comfort him, he'd lean over her shoulder and blow a raspberry at his brother, in essence saying "Gotcha!" If you remember to practice late or nonintervention, however, and only use this technique infrequently, then the few times you need this particular consequence of selective attention withdrawal, it will work.

Going Back

If everything I've said sounds too calm and reasonable to enact when you're hyperventilating because your children are fighting, keep in mind that if you blow up, saying "You! Go to your room. And you! Wait till your father gets home!" remember this: It's not necessarily what you do or say, it's what you do or say *after* what you've already done or said. After you've lost your cool, go back and tell your children that you got angry (or frustrated or upset) because you were scared, or overwhelmed with the noise, or whatever, and that you wish you had handled it differently. By apologizing for your angry outburst, you help your children learn to apologize, too (even to their siblings!) Then go through the steps of this technique after the fact. It will still be effective! And maybe the next time you'll be able to take the deep breath you need to use the technique during the conflict.

Your Role and a Word of Hope

Last, but certainly not least, remember that your intervention, your wishes, your expectations, even your presence all skew the dynamic between your children.

Many parents want so badly for their children to be friends that they intervene way too often and try to force the friendship on the children. The more you push, the more likely your children are to resist. If you can manage to step back and allow them to work things out themselves, it will, in all likelihood, bond them far more firmly than any coaxing, cajoling, or disciplining you might do.

Take this to heart: Most siblings wind up enjoying each other's company when they become adults in spite of intense rivalry when they were children, but only if we give them the room to forge their own relationship.

Chapter 12
Children and Their Grandparents

Whether Grandma and Grandpa live in the city or in a different state altogether, some people find that visiting them is a relaxing and positive experience. Maybe you get that much-needed half hour of extra sleep while Grandma feeds the kids breakfast. Or Grandpa takes the kids for a walk and you have the opportunity to begin that novel you've been dying to read all winter. On the other hand, many people find that visiting their parents causes an unexplained emotional return to adolescence, wherein they become twelve years old, tongue-tied, exasperated, and sometimes angry. This shift can be frustrating to you, not to mention confusing to your children.

"Every time I visit my mother I feel like I'm going crazy. By the second day I feel as if I can't do anything right, that I'm screwing up my children, and that I'm a terrible daughter. I'm really coming to believe that it isn't worth going, even though my kids seem to love it. I come home a wreck after only a week, and although I hate to admit it, sometimes I take out my anger and frustration on my kids after we get home. Won't it be detrimental for my kids to be exposed to the same environment that I was and which affected me negatively? Maybe I should just cut the ties and be done with it."

Maybe. Certainly there are situations in which the experience is so bad or abusive that you *should* cut the ties. In most cases, however, you might want to first examine the benefits of the grandparent-grandchild bond before making such a drastic decision.

The Benefits of the Grandparent/Child Bond

Since the beginning of history, human beings have lived in close-knit, extended-family communities where children and their parents lived at least within walking distance of grandparents, aunts, uncles, and other relatives. It is only in the quite recent past that different modes of transportation have allowed a scattering of the family, not just all over the continent but all over the world.

When it existed, the extended family system provided both physical and emotional support to its members. There was no guesswork about how to breast feed, what was "normal" in your child's development, how to raise your children. You got advice and wisdom from the elders in the family, who had been through it before. If you had to go out and work in the fields, there was always someone to watch the baby, and it didn't cost you $8 an hour. True, there were drawbacks—you probably were expected to go into the family business, and choices about education and freedom of expression simply weren't allowed, much less understood. The community had expectations about whom you would marry, and they probably were right—the selection was, obviously, limited.

Today we place a great deal of importance on individuality and independence. And there are many benefits to this. A whole world of careers and educational opportunities has opened up for individuals. People may, in fact, be happier now that they can follow their heart's desire. Perhaps, however, we've lost something too. The dynamic between a grandparent and grandchild is usually very different from that between a parent and child. Be-

cause Grandma and Grandpa don't have the responsibility of raising your child, they may be able to listen more, be more flexible,
or provide more understanding than you can about certain issues. Their love may seem more unconditional than yours. Their
wisdom may not fall on deaf ears and may, in fact, enrich your
child's life.

"I loved my grandfather. Oh, he was old and curmudgeony, and
I remember many times when he'd snap at us about one thing or
another. But I really remember him best as a wonderful man.
You know, I learned to love art because of him. After I'd moved
and started a family of my own, I took up art classes, and I used
to send him my paintings to critique. He wasn't always the most
diplomatic of souls, but it didn't matter. Even in his criticism, I felt
his love for me. His death was one of the greatest losses in my
life."

"The thing I remember most about my grandparent's house is
the smell. Grandma always had something cooking. She'd greet
us at the door and I remember being enveloped in her bosom.
She smelled like apples and cinnamon and flour, with sometimes the faintest earthy smell of the garden mixed in. She
taught me to sew and crochet, and I remember thinking I'd never
use those skills. Last Christmas, though, my daughter received
a book on making sock dolls, and I was able to sit down and
show her ladder stitches and backstitches and running stitches.
I couldn't believe that after all those years I still remembered. I
just wish Grandma was alive so I could tell her how much I appreciated her."

I realize that not all people feel this way about their grandparents.
But before you decide to cut the ties because of your own frustration, perhaps you should think about whether doing so might
be a selfish rather than a protective act on your part.

"To Grandmother's House We Go . . ."

If you have a rocky relationship with your parents but decide that you'll continue to visit them, then perhaps having some techniques under your belt that will keep your frustration level to a minimum will be useful.

Preparing Yourself

In order to thrive (not just survive) during a visit to the grandparents' house, you must prepare, prepare, and prepare some more. This doesn't mean preparing just your child but yourself as well.

If you've been to your parents' house (or in-laws' house) with your children previously, you should have a handle on what issues are likely to come up during future visits. In thinking through how things are different at your parents' or in-laws' home, you may be able to head off some of your frustrations at the pass.

"I've really worked on getting my son to listen to me. He's always been on the difficult side, and at ten, he's really struggling for independence. But I think we've finally got things under control. The problem is that I'm going to visit my father in a few weeks, and he always undermines my parenting skills. In the past, when I've asked Josh to do something, my father will say 'Leave the boy alone, he's only a kid,' and Josh will grin and I'll end up doing whatever it was that I wanted Josh to do. I feel really nervous and uncomfortable bringing this up with my dad, but at the same time, I feel like Josh and I have come such a long way, I don't want to lose the progress we've made."

In thinking through past visits with her father, Caroline, in the last example, has a relatively good handle on what might happen during this visit and how the repercussions from it might affect some recent strides she's made in her relationship with her son.

In thinking through for yourself what might come up when you visit your own parents or in-laws, try asking yourself these questions:

- Do the rules change between your house and your parents' or in-laws' house?
- What is likely to "push your buttons"? Does Grandma insist on giving chocolate to your children as snacks? Does Grandpa take the children's side when they beg to stay awake "just ten more minutes"?
- Which issues do you feel the strongest about?
- Which issues have you struggled with in your home and are the most likely to create the biggest problem when you return home?

Choose Your Battles

Once you've thought through all of the issues that are likely to arise, it's important to decide in advance what rules or issues you can be flexible with. After all, this *is* a vacation, and the rules should be a little more relaxed.

If you walk into the situation knowing that you're going to be flexible, and you know which issues are and are not negotiable, you're less likely to feel anxious and stressed once you're there. On the nonnegotiable issues, you might want to try what Caroline did.

Writing Things Down

I suggested to Caroline that maybe it would be helpful to write down how she might present her dilemma to her father, then to anticipate his reactions and write down responses to those reactions as well. When she'd done that, perhaps a friend could help her role-play by acting out the part of her father.

"I wrote everything down and asked my friend Susan to role-play with me. I have to laugh, because she made it really difficult! But I got through it, and I definitely felt more comfortable about calling my dad. Susan urged me to call right away, while everything was still fresh in my mind. So I did. I read a lot of what I wanted to say from my 'script,' and much to my surprise, he really listened. He even sounded thoughtful and concerned, and at the end of the conversation, he agreed to be careful and try to back me up during the visit when I asked Josh to help with something!"

Stepping Back

"I'm too nervous to confront my in-laws. They're really set in their ways and I know that no matter what I say, they simply won't listen."

Sometimes, whether your child's grandparents are likely to be extremely oppositional, or whether you lack the nerve to discuss these issues with them, you'll decide that you must choose a more passive route. To do so, it helps to develop an attitude that allows you to step back and permit your child to forge her own relationship with your parents (or in-laws). Remember that their perceptions of one another, their history, and the dynamics of their relationship are *by nature* different from yours. Your issues are not their issues and (in all likelihood) never will be. So while something your in-laws (or parents) do may really yank your chain, very often it passes directly over your child's head, and she remains unaffected. If the situation is likely to be very tense for you, however, you should consider planning to get away from the tension at least once a day during the trip.

Scheduling Stress-Free Time

"One thing that really helped my wife and me when we went to my parents' house was scheduling an activity that was out of the house each day of the visit. We'd stay out for a couple of hours, sometimes with the children, sometimes without, and it just helped us regroup and remember that we were adults and not still twelve years old."

In loosely scheduling a daily activity for each day during the visit, you give yourself the opportunity to regain your sense of self. In addition, many times the "free time" during a vacation becomes "stress time" because your parents or in-laws may have different expectations from yours about what happens during that free time. Scheduling an activity during free time can help.

"Free time is the worst at my parents' house. My husband is an introvert and really needs some alone time during each day. But when we're at my parents' house, we're expected to spend all of our free time 'visiting,' which mainly consists of us sitting around and staring at each other for what seems like hours on end, while the children get cranky because they're so bored. And after the children are in bed it doesn't end. If we don't stay up playing Monopoly with my parents until 11:30 at night, my mother makes snide comments about how terrific my dad was when they visited her parents, because no matter how tired he was he always stayed up and played Scrabble. Meanwhile, the tension is so thick you could cut it with a knife. Once we started planning activities during some of that 'free time,' though, things got a lot better. And it also made room for my husband to go off by himself for a little while if he needed to."

Remember that even if you've scheduled a couple of activities, if you find you're having a good time, you always can cancel your plans. But scheduling an activity gives you an "out" should you need it. Of course, be sure to tell Grandma and Grandpa beforehand about your plans so that potential conflict is avoided once you're there.

Prepare Your Child for the Visit

"We don't see my parents terribly often, simply because they live so far away. My children are very sensitive, and a little shy, so when we do visit, it takes them awhile to warm up to their grandparents. I know that it hurts my folks' feelings, but I'm not sure what to do about it."

Children of all ages and temperaments need time to process transitions. After all, they'll be going to a place where the rules are different, the dynamics are different, the faces are different. Talking to your children in advance of the visit can help ease them into this transition. In discussions you might want to:

- Sit down with your photo album where Grandma and Grandpa appear. Tell your child stories about them, including things you did on your last visit to them. Even if you're sure your child remembers his grandparents well, the storytelling will reacquaint him with their personalities and help him bring up memories of his own.
- Be sure to explain any rules that are going to be different at Grandma's house to your child thoroughly and more than once. When you're visiting and prior to your return home, explain again that the rules are different at home. This will lessen the feeling of disruption and consequently the chance of rebellion when you return.

- Discuss some of the things you're going to do while on the visit. Having an idea of the schedule often eases elementary school children's anxiety.

Talking to Your Child's Grandparents

You also might want to consider explaining to your parents or in-laws about your children's temperaments and what they can do to ease your children into the visit. Maybe reading a book as a warm-up will help, or scheduling an activity, such as going to the zoo, will help your children feel comfortable more quickly. Other children might feel more comfortable exploring the new environment a little on their own, while the adults have coffee in the kitchen. In any case, sometimes it's helpful when grandparents know what to expect from your children upon your arrival so that they don't have unrealistic expectations.

The Child Who's Visiting Grandparents Alone

"My son Jonathan adores his grandparents, who live in a different city from us. He begged us for years to visit them by himself, which would mean taking a three-hour train ride. When he turned eight, we acquiesced and agreed to the visit. He was very excited and told everyone he was going. About two weeks before he was supposed to leave, though, he began having nightmares—about train wrecks and about us disappearing. He was clearly anxious about going by himself. So I called my father, and asked if he'd come and escort our son on the train and ride back with him as well. When I told Jonathan, he got really angry, but he did seem less anxious. I'm not sure if we made the right decision or not."

Allowing your child to travel alone is a tough decision, and many parents who think their children are resourceful enough to do this find out, as Jonathan's parents did, that readiness for this kind of independence may be slower in arriving than they would have thought. Jonathan's parents did a good job in recognizing that the nightmares were anxiety related and in coming up with a different game plan for their son. His anger at their decision was probably just a way for him to save face, since his anxiety lessened as a result.

Assessing Your Child

Each child differs in his ability to handle independence. Yet all children push for independence regularly, and frequently push before they're actually ready to have it given to them. As parents, we must somehow achieve a balance between protecting our children and allowing them appropriate independence.

"My daughter, who's nine, asked to fly alone to visit her grandparents. I gave it a great deal of consideration, because she is so mature and independent and resourceful, but my final decision was 'no.' I really felt that it might stretch her resources to the limit, and I didn't want to put her in a situation where she ultimately might not be able to handle it. Of course, she ranted and raved and told me that I was treating her like a baby. She said that I didn't believe in her. I simply said, 'You know, the hard thing about being a parent is that many times your children are ready to do things before you're ready to let them. It's hard on you too, I know that. And we'll probably continue to have this dilemma as time goes on, with you always being a little ahead of me. I hope you'll be patient with me as I try to catch up with you.' She rolled her eyes and said, 'I wish you'd try to catch up a little faster.' "

This mother did a good job in explaining the dilemma that all parents face. If you're unsure as to your child's readiness, or even if you feel sure she's ready but *you* feel insecure or uneasy, then don't let your child travel alone. In my experience, many elementary school children do *not* have the internal resources for solitary travel and are better off waiting until their preteen or teenage years before being given this kind of responsibility.

Chapter 13

Your Children and Their Peers

The Influence of Peers

My daughter came home from kindergarten only a week or two after it started, slicing the air with her palms, kicking the air and yelling "HIIIIIIIIIIII-YAH!" Turning to me, she smiled and said with a gleam in her eye, "I'm going to karate the table, Mom." As I had never introduced her to the idea of "karate-ing" anything, it was clear that peer influence had begun.

For most of us, friendships are reciprocal. We influence and are influenced by friends. Our children are no different. As they make friends at school, their behavior is influenced by these friends. This is to be expected, even welcomed. The broader the range of peers, the greater our children's adaptability to different social situations.

But peer influence has a dark side as well. Many parents harbor fears that one of their children's "friends" may be exerting more influence than they feel comfortable with. Most parents would prefer that they, not peers, exert the major influence in their children's lives.

"My daughter came home from first grade about midway through the year and said, 'Mom, Sarah (a classmate whom my daughter admired at the time) said that she was having sex with her boyfriend. Mom, what does "sex" mean?" I thought I was going to faint on the spot! But I held it together, and I sat her down and told her what 'sex' meant and that children didn't have sex—not with other children and not with adults—and that it was inappropriate for Sarah to even be saying that she was having sex. My daughter looked sheepish and said, 'Mom, I didn't know that. And so after she said it, I sort of said it to a couple of my friends too.' I couldn't believe that we were already having to deal with something like this in first grade! I felt embarrassed to think that maybe some of the other first graders were going home and telling this same story to their parents, but they were reporting that *my* daughter said it. I don't want my daughter to admire some other kids so much that she says or does things just to win the other person's attention or admiration."

Self-Esteem

Remaining the major influence in your child's life means understanding how important it is that your child have high self-esteem in order to resist negative peer pressure. The degree to which you can influence your child's self-esteem will directly influence the degree to which you remain his major influence.

Self-esteem really refers to how we think about ourselves. When self-esteem is high, we feel good about ourselves, we reach out to form healthy relationships, we make good decisions, taking into consideration the values that were instilled in us by our parents. With high self-esteem we also can make good decisions independent of what our friends' or neighbors' decisions or opinions might be. In other words, we feel good enough about ourselves to resist winning admiration from others through negative behavior.

On the other hand, when self-esteem is low, we feel bad about ourselves. We sometimes fail to take responsibility for our actions, because we're afraid of "looking bad" to our peers. Sometimes low self-esteem is displayed through anxious or withdrawn behavior. Sometimes it's displayed through rebellious behavior. Children with low self-esteem seek approval from peers at almost any cost.

The Self-Esteem Pyramid

In their article "On Kids and Confidence" published by Childcraft, Stephen Garber, Marianne Garber, and Robyn Spizman describe the influences on a child's self-esteem as taking the shape of a pyramid with four levels. In this paradigm, a parent's unconditional love for and acceptance of a child forms the foundation of the pyramid. The second level is composed of the child's daily accomplishments. Level 3 involves the feedback that parents give to their children, and finally, the fourth level, or top of the pyramid, is what peers and others think of the child.

Peer influence
Parental feedback
Real accomplishments
Unconditional positive regard

When visualized this way, it is easy to see that the broader the foundation of the pyramid, the smaller the top of the pyramid is proportionally. Thus, if a parent can create a large enough base of unconditional love, peer influence will have less weight in a child's life than if the foundation of the pyramid is narrow.

Building a Strong Foundation

Expressing unconditional love and acceptance really means not confusing human Being with human Doing. With infants and small children, most parents have very little trouble expressing unconditional love based on who their child is rather than what he does. Remember, if you will, the first time you held your child in your arms and that overwhelming feeling of love that came pouring out of you. Your child didn't have to *do* anything to earn your love. It was her *Being* that created that feeling for you.

For most parents, though, it's easier to unconditionally love and accept little human Beings before they begin doing stuff. Like talking back, or breaking things, or leaving piles of dirty laundry around. And it's during the toddler years, when our children begin all this *doing*, that some parents unwittingly begin making their love conditional based on their child behaving in certain ways.

Even if you manage to get through toddlerhood without placing conditions on your love, once your child enters the school system, it becomes increasingly difficult. Upon entering school, children begin to be judged by the school "system" on the basis of their accomplishments (their *Doing*). In order to feel involved, parents may take on that judgmental attitude, believing that involvement and concern means judging their child on the same basis that the "system" does. Statements like "He's great at math, we just need to get his spelling up to par" send the message to the child that his parents are judging him based on his behavior, accomplishments, or actions rather than on *who* he is as a whole person. Suddenly the child begins to get the message that his parents' love is conditional—and the base of the self-esteem pyramid becomes smaller.

One woman asked me, "Well, what happens when our child's 'Doing' becomes their Being?" I asked her what she meant. She said, "Well, when my child comes home from school, he just starts being pesty—you know, like he starts getting into stuff, and bouncing off the walls, and taking lots of toys and stuff out without putting them back. He's just being pesty!"

This woman is confused. Her son isn't "being pesty," he's doing "pesty" things. His Being, however, is still the same as the tiny infant she once held in her arms long ago.

Sometimes, when children are very challenging, it's hard to

see their Being inside their doing. If you're having trouble with this, then walk into your child's room the next time she's fast asleep and look at her for a moment. There, lying on the bed, not doing anything, is the Being you love so much. And the next time she's awake and doing things you don't care for, close your eyes and remember that Being you saw slumbering so peacefully.

How to Express Love and Acceptance Unconditionally

In order to broaden the foundation of the self-esteem pyramid, we must recognize that it will take more than simply *feeling* unconditionally loving or accepting toward our children. Rather, we must *communicate* that love and acceptance to them so that they feel unconditionally loved and accepted by us. Some of the techniques you've already learned do this. Let's see how.

How Listening Conveys Acceptance

The first way in which we communicate unconditional love is by *listening* to our children. Children who feel listened to come away thinking that what they had to say was worthwhile. They believe that they are worthwhile, and, believing this, they feel good about themselves.

But listening is not necessarily easy because it is more than just being quiet and *hearing*. Hearing is a physical process in which the sound waves enter the auditory canal and strike the tympanic membrane causing it to vibrate and . . . well, you get the picture. Listening is different. In his book *The 7 Habits of Highly Effective People*, Stephen R. Covey says that if he had to choose the single most important thing he's learned in the field of interpersonal relations, it would be this: *"Seek first to understand, then to be understood."*

Listening means trying to *understand* our children.

The Child's World Is Different

Seeking that understanding is often difficult simply because the child's world is so different from that of the adult. Garry Landreth, author of *Play Therapy: The Art of the Relationship*, tells a story about an elementary school child (we'll call him Johnny) who was extremely challenging. So challenging, in fact, that many times the counselor at the school found it necessary to remove him from the classroom and speak to him in her office. One day he'd been particularly disruptive. She had just removed him from his classroom and arrived at her office when the principal called her on the telephone, stating that he had an emergency and could she please come to his office right away. She told Johnny to please stay in her office, she'd be right back, and then she left. Once in the principal's office, one thing led to another and before they knew it, twenty minutes had gone by. Then, the counselor remembered Johnny! This extremely challenging kid that she'd left in her office *alone* for twenty minutes! The principal, however, motioned for her to stay seated and told her that he'd call Johnny over the intercom system. So he pressed the intercom button and said, "Johnny, are you in there?" There was no response. He tried again. "Johnny! I said, are you in there?!" Still no response. As the counselor was getting up to go find Johnny, the principal tried one more time. "Young man," he said sternly, "if you're in there, you speak to me this instant!!" And Johnny's little voice floated back over the intercom system, saying "Hello, Wall."

The child's world is different from the world of the adult. To understand our children's feelings, motivations, priorities, agendas, indeed their way of looking at the world, we must, in essence, put ourselves in their shoes and must seek to understand their world. When we convey to them that we understand, we help them feel listened to, and in feeling listened to—no matter how nasty or uncomfortable or negative their feelings and thoughts are—they also feel unconditionally accepted by us.

In the Eyes of a Child

I wanted to find out what happens for children when they feel misunderstood by the adults in their lives—to see if it really affects their self-esteem. So I asked a group of elementary school children how they felt when their parents didn't understand their feelings. I got a variety of answers—all of them very similar. But two stuck out in my mind. One young boy said, "When my parents don't understand me, I feel like just yelling and screaming and tearing them to pieces." And one girl said, "I feel sad, because when my parents don't understand me, then I feel like I can't really be me."

I think the latter response in part describes the former. When children feel misunderstood, their very sense of self is shaken—they feel as if they can't really be themselves. And when their sense of self crumbles, even the tiniest little bit, then sometimes they feel like they just want to yell, and scream, and tear someone to pieces.

Empathy Conveys Understanding

We've talked quite a bit throughout this book about acknowledging our children's feelings. One of the major benefits of acknowledging feelings is that it expresses empathy. In expressing empathy, we send the message to our children that even if they feel very negative, and even if they don't like themselves very much, we still love them and can accept that they may have negative as well as positive feelings. Showing acceptance for all your child's feelings, both negative and positive, is analogous to someone handing you a quarter. You can't have it unless you take the "tails" with the "heads." The two sides of the coin simply can't be separated. Showing empathy helps your child feel wholly accepted by you because you're not trying to separate the negative from the positive.

The Second Level of the Pyramid— Real Accomplishments

The second level of the self-esteem pyramid involves the real accomplishments that your child experiences in the world. Real accomplishments are ones that are measurable by real-world standards, accomplishments that your child doesn't necessarily need your feedback on in order for them to go toward building his self-esteem.

"My daughter came home from school the other day just beaming. She told me that she'd had the best day of her whole life. When I asked why, she said, 'I finally did the monkey bars all by myself.' I could tell that she felt so proud of herself. It really gave her self-esteem a boost!"

When our children enjoy this kind of measurable success, it does give their self-esteem a boost. Because this is the second level of the pyramid, it is important to understand how you can set your child up to succeed in this area.

Recognizing Special Needs

"Ever since my daughter was a toddler, we knew that there was something different about her. She just didn't catch on to language the way other kids seemed to. She wasn't hugely behind, but enough for us to notice. We had her tested, and it was recommended that she be placed in a special school for a couple of years. What a difference that school made! We really saw her gain confidence in herself, and her language grew by leaps and bounds on an almost daily basis. By third grade, she was really ready to go to our local public school. She's been there two years now, and she's doing great."

Sometimes a child's special needs are obvious. She may be behind in language, he may have trouble holding a pencil and drawing shapes, she may not reach the physical developmental milestones at the appropriate ages. But if you have a child who is fairly average, it can be easy to overlook his special needs. And all children have special needs. These needs are based on the unique aspects of your child that make her who she is and must be recognized in order for you to put her in environments where she achieves real accomplishments.

"My son is bright, but he was failing in school. The teacher told us that when he sat with the other kids during 'meeting,' he just faded out. And when the room was noisy—which was frequently because there were twenty-nine kids in the class—he would just withdraw and start doodling on his paper. I had him tested, and he wasn't ADD [attention deficit disorder]. After a lot of thought, my wife and I decided that maybe he needed a smaller, more structured environment. So even though we really loved the school, we switched him to one that had smaller classes. Within a week, he was a different child—he was actively participating in school, the doodling went down to a minimum, and he even started doing his homework enthusiastically. The other day, after working on a math problem for a while, he looked up at me and said, 'I'm really good in school!' "

In recognizing their son's "special need" to be in a smaller, more structured environment, they gave him the opportunity to experience real accomplishments. Had these parents not been so tuned in, the situation might have gotten out of hand, affecting their son's attitude about school as well as his self-esteem.

When it's not possible (because of financial or geographic considerations) to switch a child out of a school where he isn't experiencing real accomplishments, you must look for other ways to compensate.

Working with the School

"I enrolled my son in the local school primarily because I just didn't have another option. As a single mom, I couldn't afford the private school in my area, and there's only one public school. By the middle of first grade, however, he was having problems. The other kids would egg him on—put pressure on him—to cut up and become 'class clown,' which is what he did, basically making mischief all day long. The teacher spoke with me, and told me she thought he was exceptionally bright and that his clowning was a result of boredom. So together we came up with a plan. She agreed to get a fifth-grade boy to 'mentor' him—to take him out of class once every day and teach him to play chess. Within two weeks there was a real difference. Because he was in the classroom less, it was a little more challenging to get his work done in the shorter amount of time, and because he was learning chess and being intellectually stimulated once a day, it cut down on his boredom. I could tell he felt better about himself too, because he'd come home beaming, and talking about 'this move' or 'that move' and how he'd outfoxed the fifth grader."

With the help of the teacher, this mother was able to pinpoint her son's "special need" for intellectual stimulation above and beyond the normal first-grade activities. Once he began experiencing success in the game of chess, his self-esteem rose, which helped him stand up to peer pressure and become better behaved in the classroom.

Extracurricular Advantages

Another way to give your child real accomplishments is to choose extracurricular activities in which she shows some promise.

"My daughter struggles in school, and even though she ends up with okay grades, it's hard for her. I really felt that she needed an area outside of academics in which to succeed, so I talked to her about enrolling her in dance or gymnastics because she's very physical. Neither of those appealed to her, but she suggested soccer. So I looked into it, and it turns out there's a girl's soccer league right in our neighborhood, and it's free! My daughter loves it, and she's really good—she even got voted 'most valuable player'! I've really seen a difference in her self-esteem, and it's even affecting her schoolwork—she sticks with difficult problems longer, and once when she was having trouble, she looked at me and said, 'But it's okay, Mom, 'cause I know that even if it takes me awhile, I'll eventually score the goal.' I love that she's using sports analogies to talk about academics!"

Allow Independence

Another part of "real accomplishments" includes allowing your children appropriate independence. In order to understand how important independence is to your child's self-esteem, we must first look at how its opposite—overprotection—diminishes self-esteem.

The Difference Between Protection and Overprotection

There's a fine line between protection and overprotection. As parents, it's certainly our job to protect our children from real danger or potential harm. When we protect our children, it helps them feel safe and secure, and when children have that kind of security, self-esteem can flourish. Many times, however, we protect our children from things that are not dangerous.

"My son is very responsible for a nine-year-old. He takes his schoolwork seriously and always does his homework. One night, though, he forgot to do part of his history. It was on the way to school that he remembered, and I thought he was going to have a nervous breakdown. He was so worried about what the teacher would say that I told him I'd come with him and speak to the teacher in person to let her know what happened."

When we do things for our children that they can do for themselves, we undermine their self-esteem. This nine-year-old boy, with a little encouragement, could have handled talking to his teacher on his own. When his mother took over and approached the teacher herself, she basically sent the message to her son that she didn't think he was capable of handling it himself.

Stimulating Your Child's Independence

"My daughter came home from third grade complaining about a kid in her class who was picking on her, calling her 'pig face,' standing in her way when she went to get something from her cubby, being a real bully. Well, I wanted to grab a baseball bat and go in swinging! But I knew that if I did that, I might send my daughter the message that this was something she couldn't handle on her own. So I empathized with her and said it sounded hard. Then I asked her if she could think of any way she might be able to handle it. And she said, 'Like what?' So I said, 'Well, I'm not sure myself . . . But what do you think would happen if you gave him a choice? Like maybe tell him that he can either step out of your way, or you'll ask the teacher to come over and help you work it out with him.' My daughter got this thoughtful look on her face and said, 'Ooooo, that's good, Mom! That's just like the choices we give Sam [her little brother] only Sam's more mature than this kid!' "

Now this mother did a good job. Rather than responding out of her own feelings of protection for her daughter, she correctly assessed that the girl could be empowered to handle this situation on her own. After all, while it was the first time she ever encountered a bully, it certainly wouldn't be the last. Using her listening skills to provide empathy, then asking her daughter whether she could think of any way she might handle the situation, Mom firmly established that she understood the problem and that it was her daughter's responsibility to handle it. Then she phrased some "advice" in the form of a question so that she didn't block communication and gave her daughter the resources to go back to the situation empowered. So let's see what happened the next day when her daughter came home from school.

"Well, I couldn't wait to hear what my daughter had to say the next day. The minute she got home, I followed up with her and asked how it went, whether she had felt comfortable using the choice with this boy. Her face broke into a huge grin, and she said, 'It went great! When he tried to block my cubby, I gave him the choice, and he moved right out of my way.' I asked if he bothered her again that day, and she said no. And the truth is that he really hasn't bothered her that much since then. I know she felt capable and confident because she was able to handle it on her own."

Stimulating your child's independence gives her a sense of real accomplishment that helps build her self-esteem and ultimately makes her less vulnerable to peer pressure.

When Protection Is Necessary

Obviously, protection is necessary when your child is truly in a dangerous or potentially dangerous situation. Had the bully at school been threatening this woman's daughter with a knife or even a sharp pencil, adult intervention would be required.

The Third Level of the Pyramid— Parental Feedback

As parents, we have yet another window of opportunity to influence our children's self-esteem and thus make them less vulnerable to peer pressure. This opportunity occurs in the third level of the pyramid and is determined by the feedback you give to your children. Feedback refers to the communication we enter into with our children on a daily basis. It encompasses some of the techniques we've already been talking about throughout this book—techniques of discipline, empathy, listening, and problem solving. There are three other areas of feedback that we still need to contemplate to complete the picture—instructional/corrective feedback, general vs. specific feedback, and covert feedback.

Instructional/Corrective Feedback

Much of the general feedback we give to our children is either instructional or corrective. Either we're telling them what to do and how to do it, or we're telling them what they did wrong and how to do it better next time. While instruction and correction are a necessary part of parenting, and it is our job as parents to teach our children, we must do so while building their self-esteem, not whittling away at it.

"I feel like I'm on my daughter's back all the time. It's 'Pick up this,' or 'Put away that,' or 'Have you done your homework yet?' I know that I'm not feeling good about the feedback I'm giving her, and I think it's affecting my daughter's self-esteem as well. I just see her getting deflated by the end of the day."

Being "on our kid's backs" all the time does deflate their self-esteem. One thing we can do to avoid this is to limit our nagging. The discipline techniques we've talked about can help you say things once, then act. It may also help to ask yourself this: "When my children are grown, what do I want them to remember about my interactions with them?" Do you want them to remember you as someone who was always difficult to satisfy? Or would it be better if they remembered you as someone who accepted their best efforts, even if they weren't quite perfect?

"My son cleaned up his room the other day. He spent quite a long time doing it. When he said he was finished, I came in to look. He'd done a pretty good job, but he left a few art supplies on the floor. I paused for a moment and remembered about giving positive feedback. Then I told him that I could tell he worked really hard and he'd done a good job. I gave him a hug and then I offered to help him with the last few things."

This mother did a wonderful job. She could have come in with instruction: "Pick up the markers and art supplies, too, please," or correction: "When you clean up your room you have to pay attention to details—for example, you left some markers on the floor." Instead, she chose to build on the positive, on what her son had done correctly. By offering to help with the final few things, she drew his attention to them without her feedback becoming negative.

General Feedback

Another mistake parents make when giving feedback to their children lies in making it too general. General feedback frequently occurs when we use the words "good" and "bad." For example, when your daughter cleans off the dining room table without being asked, and you give her a big hug and say "You're such a good girl," that's general rather than specific feedback. Statements that include the words "good" or "bad" don't communicate to our children which behaviors they should repeat and which behaviors they should eliminate. In addition, such statements frequently give the impression that mistakes are irreversible or catastrophic, not simply learning tools for making better choices in the future.

"I never tell my son he's a 'bad' boy. But I do tell him he's 'good' when he does something I appreciate—like finishing his homework before watching television. The other morning he suddenly remembered that he'd forgotten to do part of his schoolwork the night before. He began ranting and raving—he was really hard on himself. And he kept saying 'I'm such a bad student, I'm never going to learn. I can't believe I forgot to do my reading.' "

Even if you never use the word "bad" to describe your child, children know what the opposite of "good" is. If they've been described as a "good boy" when they do their homework, then when they forget or fail to do their homework, they automatically will think of themselves as "bad," as this boy did.

The other problem with the words "good" and "bad" is that they attach "self-worth" to behavior. Saying "good" or "bad" girl/boy is a judgment call on the child as a person rather than an attempt to promote appropriate behavior or to correct misbehavior. In addition to being the wrong kind of parental feedback to enhance self-esteem, it also violates the first premise of *unconditional love and acceptance* that forms the foundation of the self-esteem pyramid.

Specific Feedback

In order to give your child feedback that promotes high self-esteem, try making it specific rather than general. In other words, instead of telling your child what a "good boy/girl" he/she is, say specifically what you like about the behavior. For example: "I like it when you clean up your toys before getting your games out," or "Thank you for putting your dishes in the sink. I really appreciate it," or even simply "Great job!" Likewise, instead of "bad boy/girl," talk specifically about the *behavior* you want corrected.

Say "I feel uncomfortable when the toys are all over the place. I'd like you to pick them up before getting your games out," or "I feel upset when you neglect your homework. I'd like you to finish it before you watch TV."

Covert Feedback

Another influence on self-esteem within the feedback that we give our children has to do with our expectations of them. Many times these expectations, or things we think our children "should" be doing, subtly influence our feedback. Thus, while the overt messages we send our children may seem positive, the underlying or covert feedback may be negative.

"I know my son isn't terrific at sports, he really has more of an artistic nature. But I just can't help feeling that he should know something about them, or he'll feel left out with his friends. So I signed him up for a camp this summer that has an emphasis on sports. Of course, he protested mightily, but I told him that I knew he could excel if he just put his mind to it."

First of all, notice Dad's use of the word "should" when he refers to his son knowing something about sports. This word can serve as a cue that your expectations for your child may be causing negative covert feedback. Later, when Dad tells his son that he knows he'll excel if he just puts his mind to it, he may feel as if he's being encouraging. After all, he probably thinks he's saying "You can do it!" What the son probably "hears" him saying, however, is "The reason you're bad at sports is because you don't put your mind to it. Now shape up!" When our expectations for our children are unrealistic because they don't have the talent, because they don't want to participate in a particular activity, because they're not developmentally ready, or simply because our expectations are too high in general, then a you-can-do-it attitude actually can lower self-esteem instead of raising it.

Positive Expectations

While we want to avoid basing our positive expectations on the "shoulds" we have for our children, there are ways that positive expectations can work to the benefit of high self-esteem.

Most parents today recognize that negative labels (such as "accident-prone") become a self-fulfilling prophecy. Used often enough, the child who is called "accident-prone" can become "accident-prone." Many parents, however, fail to realize that just as children live up to negative expectations, they also live up to positive expectations. But in order for positive expectations to work for high self-esteem, you must know what it is reasonable to expect from your children. The best way to know this is to buy a book on developmental levels appropriate for your child's age. An ideal series of books that I highly recommend comes from the Gesell Institute. Each book is entitled according to the age of the child—*Your Five-Year-Old, Your Six-Year-Old,* and so on.

When children are infants, most parents keep a reference book around to help them understand the changes that children go through. Once the children reach school age, however, parents drop this practice. But developmental levels are not restricted to infancy. Children pass through different stages all the way up to and through adolescence, and knowledge of these stages is critical for parents who are interested in building self-esteem. Once you've determined the stage your child is in, set realistic goals for her and keep your expectations positive about her achievement of those goals. It's important, however, to balance this attitude of "You can do it!" with an acceptance of her possible failure.

Part Three

Your Child's World

Chapter 14

"My Child Stole Something (and Then Lied to Me)!"

$\mathbf{M}$y six-year-old daughter, Lisa, took a necklace from her friend. When she got home, I saw the necklace and asked her where she'd gotten it. She said that her friend gave it to her. I didn't give it another thought. Later, my daughter's friend and her mother showed up at our door and asked if Lisa had taken the necklace. It was then that Lisa admitted that she'd stolen it. I'm still completely shaken and totally shocked."

Many elementary school-age children experiment with stealing and lying for the first time during these seemingly innocent years. That this type of behavior occurs should surprise us no more than any other type of "testing." Yet somehow, when our children steal or blatantly lie for the first time, it can be an intensely emotional experience. How, after all, could they have done something that so contradicts our own values? Furthermore, what on earth should we do about this kind of behavior?

Instilling honesty in your child involves three basic components: role-modeling honesty, setting yourself (and your child) up for success, and handling dishonest behavior.

Role-Modeling Honesty

I think most of us believe that we lead moral, honest lives. And that's probably a true statement. What we fail to realize, however, is that honest, ethical behavior is not at all black and white but has many, many shades of gray. Sometimes we pass off the "white lies" we tell or the small, petty dishonesties in which we engage as ethical. Yet are they? And do they go unnoticed by our children? I think not. Further, I think it's very likely that not only do our children notice the "little dishonesties," but they mimic them, using us as role models, when a situation that they encounter parallels one they've seen us handle as adults. To see what I mean, take a moment and answer the following questions. As you do, remember that they have no right or wrong answers. Please answer as honestly as possible, avoiding the temptation to write an answer down because you think it's what you "should" do. The answers you give are merely intended to provide insight into your values and help you understand the development of your child's values.

- Your Aunt Martha invited you to dinner on Friday and you accepted the invitation. Meanwhile, the kid's soccer game was rescheduled due to rain for that same Friday. You know your aunt won't accept this as an excuse, but you really want to go to the game. Would you tell her that you don't feel well on Friday so you can attend the soccer game?
- Your child has been waiting for weeks to see a special program on television. On the day that the program is scheduled to air, a special news report preempts his program. He learns that the program he wants to watch has been rescheduled for the following day, during school. Can he say he's sick and can't go to school because he wants to watch the TV program? (You don't own a VCR.)

- You're at the office and your pen runs out of ink. You go to the stockroom and pick up a box of pens for your desk. Later you remember that you're also out of pens at home. Would you take a few from the office since they have so many?
- Your child is drawing a phenomenal picture at home. He's almost done, but he discovers he's used up the red colored pencil that he needs to complete the project. Rats! He goes to bed with the artwork unfinished. The next day, at school, he notices that the exact color pencil he needs is right there. Can he take it home to complete his picture?
- You're at the grocery store, and you notice that there's a $10 bill on the floor. Would you take it or give it to the cashier?
- Your child is at school and notices that there's a quarter on the floor near the teacher's desk. Should he take it or should he give it to the teacher?
- You notice that your boss is "manipulating numbers" on a report. When you confront him about it, he refuses to stop, and insists that if you report it to his boss, he'll make sure you lose your job. Would you tell his boss?
- Your daughter notices her brother cheating on his homework—he's getting the answers from a friend. She tells her brother that she saw him and asks him to stop, but her brother refuses. Further, he threatens that if she tells you about it, he'll "pound" her. Should she tell you?

These are hard questions, and they either have no answer, or the answer varies depending on your individual values. The purpose is to allow you to see the parallel issues that children and adults face, to make you aware and thoughtful about what your children see you role-modeling for them. Keep in mind that how our children will act when faced with these situations is, in part, determined by how they've seen us act in what they believe are similar situations. As you continue reading, remember that the first way in which we support our children's development of honesty is by being a good role model.

Setting Yourself (and Your Child) Up for Success

One of the most interesting things about parenting is that most parents actually spend relatively little time talking about the importance of something like ethical behavior, and yet they still expect their children to become honest, ethical adults.

In order for our children to get the sense that we value honest behavior, not only must they see us being honest, but they must hear us talking about the benefits of honesty. At most, parents may comment casually on the value of ethical behavior as an aside to another conversation, when it would be far more beneficial if children could hear us talking about it in depth and frequently. In order to talk about it and help our children recognize its importance, we must first have a deeper understanding of its worth.

"I told my daughter that one good reason to be honest was that it makes us feel good inside. I recounted a time when I had stolen something as a kid—it was a soda from a gas station, and I drank it quickly in the bathroom. I didn't get caught, but I remember going home and just feeling awful inside, like there was a big, ugly, brown hole inside of me. I told her that it felt like something heavy was on my chest. She looked at me with wide eyes and asked what happened. So I told her the truth, that the guilt was too much, and I went and told my parents. I got in a lot of trouble, and had to go back and face the manager of the gas station, but I felt so much better. It was like the hole in me went away, and even though I was in trouble, I felt better about myself."

I think in general we do feel better about ourselves when we tell the truth, because it gives us a sense of personal integrity. This father did a great job talking with his daughter, not only about his personal experience with dishonesty but in creating concrete images like "a big, ugly, brown hole inside" that she could relate to. The more that you can sprinkle your discussions with visual images, the more likely your child will be able to relate to the story and learn from it.

In talking to your own child about the importance you place on honest behavior, you also might want to include the concept that when you're honest, people are more likely to trust you, and when you're trusted, you have more freedom and privileges.

Catch Your Child Doing It Right

Another powerful motivator involves talking about honest behavior when your child has behaved honestly. Many parents make the mistake of reacting only when they catch their children doing something wrong. This sends the message to them that no matter how much they do that we approve of, they'll get attention only when they behave inappropriately. In the case of honesty, they wind up feeling that it's not worth it to be honest, because we never comment on that.

When your child admits to a misbehavior at school, catch her doing it right and say, "I really appreciated that you told me what happened at school today. That might have been a little difficult for you to say, and you might not have known how I'd react. I appreciate your honesty, and I feel as if I can trust you." This attitude of "catch them doing it right" is a powerful lesson, because children learn that we're paying attention *all* of the time, not just when they're dishonest.

Building Your Child's Courage

Another way to set yourself up to succeed in developing an ethical child is to devote time and energy to building your child's courage. Let's face it, sometimes it's really difficult to be honest, because the consequences can range from unpleasant to down-right nasty. We've already talked about raising self-esteem and building courage in other chapters, but let's do a quick review.

- We build courage in our children's daily lives when we separate who they are from what they do. We constantly must send the message to our children that we may not love what they do, but we'll always love who they are. If our children live in fear of losing our love, they will lie whenever they're afraid that we'll be mad about what they did. Children who feel unconditionally loved and accepted are far more likely to risk our anger, because they know that no matter what happens, we'll still love them. The message to our children must be that while we may get angry, we still love them.
- Another way to build courage is by showing confidence in your child. When we trust our children to be honest, and convey that confidence to them, they will live up to our trust. It's far more powerful to say "I believe in you. I believe you'd tell me if you did something wrong. I trust you" than to say "Are you sure you're telling me the truth? It doesn't sound like it to me. Look at your face, it has 'lie' written all over it. Now out with it! What really happened?"
- Lunch box/backpack notes build courage on a systematic basis. When we promote honesty in the family, we increase the likelihood that our children will come to us with the truth. But even if you're promoting honesty in your family, undoubtedly there will be times when your child will lie to you.

Our Response to Dishonesty

When our children lie to us, it's almost like getting slapped in the face, and it leaves us shocked, confused, and often very angry.

Frequently our response to those feelings of frustration, anger, and helplessness is to become punishing. We withhold privileges, we yell, and we threaten, among other things, in hopes of scaring them into telling us next time.

"My son came home from school and said that he'd decided to quit chorus. I was surprised, but he said he was bored and overwhelmed with other things, so I didn't push it. But then I heard from his teacher that he didn't quit, he'd been kicked out because he was so disruptive. Well, I saw red!! I called him in to where I was and started yelling 'I can't believe you'd lie to me! What's the matter with you? If I ever catch you in a lie again, I'll come down on you so hard you won't know what hit you. Now go to your room—you're grounded for the month.' That ought to make an impression!"

Undoubtedly this father's response *will* make an impression. The question is, what kind? Within this communication, what his child is the most likely to hear is *"If I ever catch you in a lie again, I'll . . ."* With this beginning, you can be sure that next time it *won't* be as easy to catch him, especially if he has anything to say about it!

You see, when we respond to our children's misbehavior (in this case lying) by yelling at and threatening them, we make ourselves even less approachable in the future. Yelling, threatening, and punishing are self-defeating, because what we *want* is for them to feel comfortable coming to us with the truth. Somehow, we must find a balance between teaching them a lesson about lying and making them comfortable about coming to us in the future with the truth.

So what do we do? How can we teach our children a lesson yet still keep the lines of communication open so they aren't afraid to come to us in the future when a difficult situation arises?

Two Types of Lies

First of all, let's distinguish two types of lies and what motivates our children to tell them.

One kind of "lie" is the fanciful storytelling that is so common among younger children. For example: "Mommy, today at school a guy with a big bag over his shoulder came into the schoolyard. And he handed out presents to all the kids, because he was really Santa Claus. But I didn't get a present, 'cause I was in the bathroom when it happened." Young elementary school children are more likely to engage in this type of "lie" than older ones.

The primary motivation of most children who tell fanciful stories, no matter what their age, is to get attention. You might notice, for instance, that your child is more likely to tell this type of "tall tale" when you're busy and can't focus on her, or when another child is telling you an interesting story that you're paying attention to.

Another type of lie is when children say something that's untrue when they know that it's untrue—for example, when they say "Yes, I ate my carrots" when in reality they fed them to the dog.

Children tell untruths either to avoid punishment or because they lack the courage to approach the parent with the truth.

Helping our children to tell the truth instead of lying requires that we have a plan and know ahead of time how we'll handle the different types of lying when they come up. Distinguishing the type of lie is the first step in helping children see the benefit to telling the truth.

Handling Fanciful Storytelling

It's important to distinguish between young children and older children when we make decisions about how to handle the fanciful storytelling category of lying. For children who are in early elementary school (kindergarten through second grade), making up stories about imaginary friends, events, or encounters is a natural part of their creative development and should be treated accordingly.

"My daughter, who's in kindergarten, has an imaginary friend named Coco that she's had since she was a toddler. One day I came in to the living room after school, and I found her drawing all over herself with a Magic Marker. 'Honey,' I said, 'the paper is for drawing on, not your skin.' 'I didn't do it,' my daughter replied, 'Coco did it!' So I thought for a minute, and then I said, 'Well, you have to be responsible for Coco. Tell Coco she's not allowed to draw on anything but the paper.' "

This mother correctly assessed that "lying" in this case was a part of her daughter's natural development. Rather than make an issue out of the "lie," she simply incorporated her daughter's fantasy play into her response. Making the child take responsibility for Coco taught her child that she's not responsible only for herself but for her imagination as well.

Sometimes children this age will make up stories to get attention.

"My son came home after school one day and said, 'It was scary at school today. When we were out at recess, a man came into the schoolyard with a gun. He pointed it at all of us, and we ran inside.' I knew that it couldn't have happened, because I think the school would have called. On the other hand, I didn't want to contradict him, because I didn't know for sure what happened."

In instances like this, it's important that we take our children seriously. You might say something like "That does sound scary. Let's call your teacher. I need to find out what happened after you went inside." If your child is making it up, he will protest and ask you not to call. In that event, you might say something like "You know, sometimes when we've had a boring day, and we wish it had been more exciting, we add things that didn't really happen. It seems like that's kind of what happened to you today." If you do this, you won't put your child in a position where he has to "save face." If he feels his "reputation" is on the line, it will only cause him to dig deeper into the story. Give him a way to extricate himself gracefully. Later, be sure to address the principle of telling the truth without going into the specific instance. Say something that conveys trust "Mommy/Daddy takes you very seriously because I trust you. I believe what you tell me, and that's why it's very important to tell me when you're using your imagination, and when something really happened."

The older the child, the more concern is warranted with this type of lying. If older children (third through fifth or sixth grade) weave fantasy into many or all of their conversations, it may be important to have them evaluated to determine if they actually can distinguish reality from fantasy. There may be a psychological or physiological reason for this behavior that should be dealt with.

Keep in mind, however, that if your older child only occasionally engages in this type of lie, and it's clear that he is perfectly capable of distinguishing reality from fantasy, then it's likely that he is seeking attention in an inappropriate manner. One way to handle this is by not giving him what he's after. Keep your reaction to the story minimal; a simple "I see, well that's interesting" should do it. Later, go back to your child and address the issue of attention getting. You might try saying something like "I wonder if you feel as if you're not getting enough of my attention sometimes. I thought maybe we could talk about different ways you could get my attention when you're feeling lonely or left out." While an occasional child might question your motive for bringing this subject up, it's more than likely that most will feel a sense of relief in having their feelings recognized and in knowing that you want to address the issue. Sometimes the child will deny needing attention or having lonely feelings. That's okay. Remember that the important thing is that your child hear your willingness to address this issue even if he's not comfortable talking about it yet.

Handling the Telling of "Untruths"

When a child tells her parents an "untruth"—that is, she says something that's untrue when she knows it's untrue—it's the parents' job to determine why the child is lying. Is the child afraid of punishment because she's been punished severely before? Or is the child not sure what may happen if she tells the truth, so she is avoiding taking responsibility for what she's done?

"My daughter was supposed to go on a school trip with her class. She was very excited to have been invited. As the date approached, however, she appeared more and more reluctant to go. One week prior to the trip, there was a meeting for the parents whose children were going. When the date of the meeting arrived, my daughter begged me not to go. She said that she didn't want to go on the trip anyway. Something sounded suspicious, so of course I went, even though my daughter cried. When I arrived, I discovered that my daughter had misbehaved in class and had been told she couldn't go on the trip after all. Can you imagine how embarrassed I was to find out in front of all the other parents like that? When I got home, I was furious, and I told my daughter, 'Get over here right now. Why in the $%@!* didn't you tell you'd gotten kicked out of that trip? What's the matter with you anyway? You're really gonna be punished for this one!' Of course, she immediately burst into tears and told me that she didn't do anything, that she asked the teacher to take her off the list, and that she didn't even want to go in the first place."

This is a classic example of an "untruth." First of all, the daughter lied by omission—she withheld information from her father, probably because she was afraid of what he might do or say, and not knowing what might happen, she simply tried to avoid the situation by not telling him. When he returned home from the meeting and was so angry, she lied overtly to avoid what she clearly saw as a severe punishment to follow.

Before I discuss how Dad could handle this situation so that his daughter would understand the consequences of lying to him as well as feel comfortable coming to him in the future when she'd misbehaved in school, let me say a word about punishment and consistency.

- Punishment is defined as any retaliatory action on the part of the parent, either physical or emotional, that is intended to teach children to behave obediently by making them feel bad or by hurting them. Many times punishment isn't terribly logical, and parents often use one punishment for many different types of misbehavior. For example, a parent might use spanking as a primary disciplinary tool and might spank a child for a variety of misbehaviors, from pulling the cat's tail to stealing. When children are punished in this way, they soon learn to avoid the punishment by withholding information and feelings from their parents. Research indicates that physical punishment or harsh nonphysical punishment *increases* rather than decreases a child's tendency to lie.

- Consistency: In the last scenario, the daughter withheld information from her father because she didn't know what to expect in terms of his reaction. Most often, this is caused because as parents, we're not terribly consistent about how we handle our children's misbehavior. If we're feeling stress-free and enjoying our child, and the child misbehaves, we chalk it up to "Well, she's a kid, after all, and kids sometimes get into trouble." If we're under stress and feeling annoyed at our child to begin with, however, our reaction is more likely to be "You get over here, right now, young lady, I've had it with you!"

This type of inconsistency causes feelings of uncertainty within children. They don't know what to expect from us, so it's kind of like walking through a minefield. They're not sure when they'll step on a land mine and be blown to smithereens. When this is the case, children have a tendency to "walk on eggshells" around their parents, never admitting to too much or too little, always watching to see what their parents might do *this* time rather than being honest and open all the time. As you work with the issue of honesty, it will be important that you make your reactions to your children's misbehavior neither too strong nor too weak. When you're consistent about your reactions, tone of voice, and the consequences for lying, your children will know what to expect, and they'll feel more comfortable about taking responsibility for their actions.

With this in mind, let's talk specifically about how to handle telling lies.

A Model for Handling the Telling of "Untruths"

1. Confront your child. Say "I want to talk to you about the school trip. Is now a good time, or should we make an appointment?" Giving your child a choice about the timing helps bring down your child's defenses. When you say "Get in here right now!" the child is immediately on the defensive and is likely to lie further.
2. Avoid name-calling. "You're a liar" decreases a child's self-esteem, while "You lied to me" keeps her self-esteem intact. Children with low self-esteem feel they can't do anything right, including being honest!
3. Say how you feel. "I feel very disappointed that you misbehaved in class and you're not being allowed to go on the trip. What concerns me even more, however, is

why you didn't come to me in the first place." Be careful to phrase it in terms of "I feel . . ." rather than "You make me feel . . ." Again, if you want your child to be more honest, it's important that she not feel attacked. While you may be *very* angry and upset, remember that your goal is long term (creating a more honest child and a more approachable parent) rather than simply short term (punishing her for this particular instance).

4. Allow your child input. Say "I'd like to hear what you have to say about all this," then listen without interrupting. This may be very difficult, because your child may meander around, fictionalize, and weave more lies into her "untruth." Allowing her to speak without interrupting, however, accords her dignity and respect, and a child who doesn't have to fight for those two things is a child who will ultimately be more truthful. To determine when your child is finished, ask: "Are you finished? May I speak now, or do you have more to say?" If she has more, listen again, until she's talked out.

5. Talk about earning trust. Say something like "Trust is something very precious and it's something you earn. The more honest you are, the more I trust you, and the more things I'll let you do, because you earned that right. When you're dishonest, however, some of my trust in you goes away, and it takes a long time to rebuild it. Now you'll have to prove to me that you can be trusted again before I can give you more responsibility or privileges." While you should tailor this to your child's age in terms of the vocabulary you use, this fact is extremely important to emphasize if your child continues to deny the lie or misbehavior. The more you lie, the more trust you lose.

6. Give a consequence. This is probably the most difficult part of how to handle your child's lies, because it's important that the consequence you give be related to the

lie. In the last case, a related consequence might be that you will check with the child's teacher on a daily basis for two weeks with regard to after-school activities, classroom behavior, and so on. If the child can prove within that time-frame that she has come home with correct information about her daily behavior and activities, then your trust will be restored. Remember to take the time to think through what the consequence for your child will be. Arbitrary, inconsistent, or overly severe consequences compound lie-telling.

Stealing

"My daughter and I went to the store together, where she saw this little book that she wanted for one of her dolls. I told her 'no' because her birthday was coming and said I might get it for her then. She seemed to be okay with that, and we got home with no incidents. When the weekend came, though, she was going to stay overnight at a friend's house, and she said, 'Mom, don't go into my doll corner, okay?' I didn't make any connection, so I just shrugged and said, 'Okay.' When she got to the friend's house, she reminded me not to go into that corner, and I began to get suspicious. But I honored her wishes, although I made a mental note to talk with her about it once she got home. Sure enough, when she got home after the weekend, she asked me again if I'd gone into the doll corner. I said no, but I also said, 'It sounds like you're concerned about that.' She said, 'No, not really,' but she had a funny look on her face. So I proceeded by saying 'I see you're thinking about something. Maybe we could discuss it.' Well, then the floodgates opened, and she admitted to having taken the little book from the store."

Whether your child tries to hide something she's stolen from you, or whether you find something she couldn't have bought among her things, your approach should be similar to how you handle her "untruths." In this scenario, Mom used listening skills to open communication rather than direct confrontation because she wasn't sure about exactly what was going on. Let's see what happened next.

"I told my daughter that I had a couple of feelings about this. On the one hand, I was proud that she had the courage finally to tell me what happened. On the other hand, I was shocked and disappointed that she would take something, knowing how very wrong it was to do."

Mom is doing a good job here. She's open about all her feelings, and she's being frank about the fact that stealing is wrong.

"I asked my daughter if she had anything to say. Well, she was crying, of course, and she said she was sorry. Then she asked what was I going to do to her. I told her that I'd talk about the consequences, but asked if there was anything else she wanted to say before I took a turn. She shook her head no."

Here Mom listens and lets her daughter speak, then asks if she has anything else to say. While this child didn't say much, some will speak for much longer. Remember to be patient—you'll get a turn too.

"Then I said, 'I love the fact that we can tell each other anything. When you do something like this, though, I feel as if I can't trust you as much as I used to. Trust is very important to me, and we'll have to figure out a way for you to earn my trust back. That may take a little time. Meanwhile, I think that your consequence should be that we have to go back to the store manager, and you have to hand him the book and tell him what happened.'"

Mom did a great job. She included a litlte information about trust and gave a logically related consequence for her daughter's stealing the book. Later she can determine how her daughter will win her trust back or if it will simply be a matter of time. In any case, she should come back and say, at some point, that trust has been restored, whether it takes a day, a week, a month, or longer.

Chapter 15
Taming the Holiday Monsters

When the weather begins to turn cold, the stores begin to decorate in red and green, and television begins to advertise the newest "craze" in toys just right for the holidays, many parents watch with dismay as their normally loving, appreciative children are slowly transformed into greedy, insatiable monsters.

Who Is This Child?

"I know this may sound extreme, but after the experience we had at Hanukkah this year, we've decided to break with tradition and not give a gift a night again. The first night our son was appreciative, but as the days wore on, he became more and more demanding, beginning early each day to question 'Where's my present?' He pestered us unmercifully! I'm simply not going through that again!!"

"At Christmas last year, my in-laws came to visit. I don't know if it was because my daughter was overly excited or what, but I was horrified when we began to open presents, because she ripped them open one after another without even taking a breath, tossing each new thing aside as if it was just so much trash. Afterward, instead of feeling full of the holiday spirit and the joy of giving, I felt embarrassed, angry, and sad."

For many parents, this type of experience can contribute to a serious case of the postholiday blues. And this phenomenon is not limited to Christmas and Hanukkah either. It also includes birthday celebrations and other occasions where presents are anticipated.

Why Do Children Behave This Way?

What makes our children behave this way? How can the child who was hugging and kissing and thanking you for buying him a pack of gum last week be the same child who, today, cavalierly tossed the $200 Nintendo set you bought him aside and demanded his next gift? Furthermore, is there anything we as parents can do to prevent our children from becoming monsters? Or are we consigned to altering or eliminating our holiday traditions in hopes of minimizing our children's greediness?

Fortunately, there is an explanation for our children's behavior, and there are things we can do to correct it.

Understanding Your Child

For most children, the excitement of a holiday or birthday celebration opens up new horizons. Suddenly those toys and that attention that they've been thinking about all year are within reach. A celebration with gifts usually means that the possibilities are endless—and perhaps the gifts will be too! With the whole world suddenly within reach, it's understandable that your child's eyes would begin to shine with excitement, and he would begin to ask about or look forward to his gifts in an overly enthusiastic manner.

In addition, most children's sense of time is distorted—even through adolescence. It's not only hard for them to delay gratification, but hard in a purely conceptual sense to understand the timing of gifts. So when they're confronted with a pile of gifts, it's even hard to admire one before opening the next. Likewise, on holidays where everyone receives gifts, waiting until Mom or Dad opens a gift and admires it before they take a turn and open one can feel like forever.

While this provides an explanation for our children's behavior, I don't think it justifies it. Lack of appreciation for gifts is inexcusable as far as I'm concerned. Understanding what makes our children operate the way they do is, therefore, only part of the story. Correction of this behavior and teaching our children to behave appropriately and appreciatively is important too.

Reframe the Situation

In order to effectively teach your child to appreciate the gifts he's given, first you must get a handle on your own feelings. Sometimes, through understanding your child's behavior, you can reframe the situation—in other words, you can change the label you give to your child's behavior. In doing so, your feelings also may change. So, instead of labeling your children's behavior as "greedy," call it "overly enthusiastic" or "overly excited" instead. Most parents have an easier time handling an overly excited child than a "greedy" one. Likewise, your feelings probably will be more generous toward an overly excited child than they are toward a "greedy spoiled brat." Once your feelings are in check, it's easier to approach the teaching of appreciation in a more systematic manner.

Give the Holiday Significance

In order for children ultimately to internalize your values about gift giving and receiving, they must come to understand the meaning behind the giving of gifts. This means examining the significance of the celebration, whether it's a birthday or a religious holiday.

"Birthdays are really important to me. I think that birth is such a miracle, it should be celebrated as such. I want my daughter and son to understand that we celebrate that miracle by giving gifts on birthdays, and that each gift is a way of saying 'I'm really glad you were born. I'm glad you came into my life.'"

Talking with your child about the significance and meaning of each holiday is the key element here. She must hear it time and time again before she can truly internalize this value. With birthdays, you can talk about the "story" of your child's birth or adoption, the first moments when you looked into her eyes, and the significance of having her enter your life.

When you're discussing religious holidays with your child, you may want to explain the religious tradition and history surrounding that holiday. If you aren't terribly religious but do celebrate the holiday, you might want to talk in more general terms—about why we give gifts and about love. Remember that your child may need a concrete explanation as well as a more abstract one; you may want to read him a story about the holiday or have him act it out himself or with dolls to understand its significance in addition to talking with him about the "spirit" of giving and the feelings that prompt us to give gifts.

The Importance of Ritual

"In our house, we've established a ritual for opening gifts—no matter what the occasion is. The person receiving the gift has to sit on the couch. If more than one person is receiving a gift, children sit on the couch, and adults sit in chairs. One person hands the gifts out one at a time, and each person opens their gift before another person starts on theirs. We began this back when the kids were really young, and now that they're ten and seven years, if someone even unexpectedly brings a gift home, they scramble onto the couch to receive it. It really cut down on the chaos."

Establishing a ritual for opening gifts is extremely helpful. If you don't have a ritual in place, invite the children to participate in coming up with one. Perhaps, for example, recycling is important in your house. You can incorporate this by saying that when you open gifts, you'll take the paper off carefully and fold it so it can be recycled. Then maybe each person can take a turn opening a gift while everyone else watches.

Voicing Your Expectations

Many children behave the way they do because they don't know what we expect them to do differently. If we don't voice our expectations about opening gifts ahead of time, then our children's enthusiasm can get out of hand. Establishing a ritual can, in part, take care of this. In addition, you also might want to tell your child *how* to show appreciation for a gift.

"When my child was in kindergarten, I couldn't stand his lack of appreciation any more. Instead of yelling at him, though, I sat him down and told him that when he opens a gift, I want him to say 'Thank you' to the person who gave it to him. If that person isn't present, I said I'd like him to wait before opening the next gift while we write down what the first gift was and who it's from so we can send a thank-you card. He nodded his head seriously, and he's really good at remembering. I guess I had just assumed that he knew how to show appreciation without my telling him how."

When You Need to Discipline

"I've tried to establish a ritual and to let my child know what I expect, but it just doesn't seem to be enough. I really dread any holiday with gifts because I always wind up feeling overwhelmed and sad about his behavior afterward."

Some children have more trouble than others with postponing immediate gratification—even long enough to say thank you. If your child is having this kind of difficulty, recognize his feelings before you use discipline. Say "You seem really excited about your birthday (Christmas, Hanukkah). Getting gifts can be overwhelming, and it can be very hard to appreciate one before going on to another." Sometimes all your child needs is to feel understood regarding his excitement about the holiday. In recognizing his feelings, you are, in effect, saying "I understand how you feel." Many times this in itself will stop the frantic ripping open of gifts or other misbehavior.

If this empathetic statement doesn't change your child's behavior, however, and you're beginning to feel annoyed, don't be afraid to set a limit with your child, even if it *is* a holiday.

"I felt that my daughter was really out of control at her birthday party, so I gently pulled her aside and said quietly, 'When you rip your gift open without thanking the child who brought it for you, I feel embarrassed, because it's unappreciative. I would like you to remember to thank each child once you've opened their gift.' "

Many parents feel hesitant to use "I" messages and/or consequences because of the celebratory nature of the holiday. Remember that these are teaching tools, and what better time to teach your child about appropriate behavior than when he's exhibiting inappropriate behavior?

"At Christmas my husband and I like to open the gifts by taking turns so that everyone can not only appreciate their own gifts but can see the appreciation other family members have for what they receive. Last Christmas, though, the kids weren't waiting for their turns, so we gave them an 'I' message, which did nothing. We stayed really calm, though, and told them that they could either wait patiently for their turn to open a present, or they could skip their turn. Both kids straightened up and chose to take turns after that."

Sometimes consequences are extremely helpful in reminding your children just what your values are about showing appreciation. When using consequences, of course, just be sure that you don't make an empty threat, such as "Be patient or we'll throw the rest of your gifts away." Because you won't follow through on the threat, you won't teach your child anything about appropriate behavior, and he'll probably rebel or throw a tantrum.

Holiday Myths

"We don't have a problem with discipline or showing appreciation during the holidays, but we celebrate Christmas, and our daughter, who's eight, still believes in Santa Claus. I kind of thought she'd have outgrown it by now, and we're not sure when we should tell her the truth."

The Importance of Myth

For many of us, the mythical characters of Santa Claus, the Tooth Fairy, the Easter Bunny, and the Sandman sprinkle our own childhood memories and fill us with nostalgia. As parents, most of us weave these fantasies into tales that enrich and enhance our own little one's childhood experience. Children eagerly look forward to the magical appearance of gifts under a tree, money under a pillow; even tales of the Sandman serve their purpose in gently transitioning a child from the excitement of a day filled with activity to a restful sleep. These mythical characters add magic and excitement to our children's lives and ultimately aid in the development of their imagination. At some point, however, most children are ready to give up their belief in Santa or the Tooth Fairy and to hear the "truth"—that these are really myths, and Mom or Dad has been playing the leading role in this fantasy play. But how do we know when that time comes?

Developmental Readiness

Most children give up on the idea of Santa, the Tooth Fairy, and other myths somewhere between the ages of four and eight years. This happens because sometime around five years of age, children develop the ability to distinguish between reality and fantasy. With that developmental leap the child begins to ask questions about the characters we've worked so hard to develop and maintain. These questions mark the child's transition from belief to disbelief. So "Mommy, is there *really* a Santa Claus?" or "Daddy, is the Tooth Fairy *real*?" may catch us by surprise but are by no means inconsistent with normal child development.

Your Response

If you're like most parents, these questions cause you to stammer and stutter, not completely sure of what to answer. After all, saying yes is a lie, but by saying no, you're choosing to end a tradition that has contributed much enjoyment and excitement to your child's as well as your own life. In essence, you're caught in an awkward bind.

The question to ask yourself is if you think your child really is ready to stop believing. In assessing this, it's helpful to know that just because a child asks a question, it doesn't necessarily mean that she is ready to hear the answer. Sometimes the question is asked simply because the child wants to make sure that it's okay to continue to believe in Santa or the Tooth Fairy. Obviously if your child isn't ready to know that these mythical characters aren't real, you shouldn't deprive her of the opportunity to keep believing.

To attempt to ascertain the extent of your child's readiness, answer her question with one of your own. Simply respond "What do you think?" Your child's reply may range from "I think there is a Santa" to "No, I think you're really the Tooth Fairy." If your child answers with something along the lines of "I'm not sure," then she's probably not ready to give up believing.

"My seven-year-old son's tooth fell out when we were in the car on the way home from school. As he was enthusiastically tucking it away in his backpack to put it under his pillow later, he suddenly stopped, looked at me, and asked, 'Dad, is there really a Tooth Fairy?' So I said, 'What do you think?' Then he threw me because he said, 'What I think doesn't matter, I want to know the *truth!*' I was so rattled I didn't know what to say next—was he ready or not ready to hear about the myth?"

As children enter the developmental stage where suspicion replaces unquestioning belief, they sometimes won't tolerate questions in answer to their questions, often making statements such as 'I want to know what *you* think' in a frustrated voice. While this alone doesn't necessarily indicate readiness to hear the truth, it's certainly important to acknowledge the seriousness of the statement. You might say "You sound pretty serious." Then if the child pursues the topic and indicates that he is serious about knowing, it's probably because he's ready to know. At this point, avoiding the answer or dancing your way around it and not answering directly may do more harm than good. Children need open, honest communication to maintain healthy family relationships. If it's clear that your child is serious about knowing, you can say "Well, Santa (or the Tooth Fairy) is just pretend. Sometimes it's fun to make believe." You could also say "The Tooth Fairy is a way to

celebrate you losing your teeth—which is a sign that you're growing up," or "The spirit of Santa is real. It's the spirit of giving, of caring about others."

When We Guess Wrong

"I think we blew it with my seven-year-old daughter. She was really pushing to know about whether Santa was real, and we vac-
illated back and forth about telling her. Finally, she pushed so
hard that we decided she was serious and ready to hear the truth.
So we sat down and went through the whole thing about the
'spirit' of Christmas, and the celebration, etc., etc., and she was
horror-stricken! It was very clear once we'd gotten partially
through that we'd incorrectly assessed her readiness, but we were
beyond the point of no return. I feel terrible!"

Some children do respond this way, and it's a difficult feeling for
parents to have gotten partway through and realize there's no
turning back. As in all things where your child appears to be having strong feelings, focusing on her emotions will be helpful and
also may help you take your foot back out of your mouth!

"A similar situation happened to us, only with the Tooth Fairy.
Actually, my husband saved the day, because he remembered to
focus on my daughter's feelings, and said, 'Sounds like this news
is a little more than you planned for. Looks like you're having
some strong feelings about it.' My daughter began to cry, and my
husband stuck with it and said, 'Seems like your feeling sad
about not believing anymore,' to which she nodded her head. He
then went on to say 'I wonder if it's helpful to know that these are
things we can choose to continue to believe in. Believing does
make things fun sometimes, and it's a choice you could make, if
you wanted to.' She kind of looked at him in amazement and
said, 'Really? I mean, I can still choose to believe in it, even if it's
not true?' And he said yes. Since that day, which was a year and

a half ago, she's steadfastly maintained her belief in *all* the myths, except the Sandman, which she gave up when she was five."

Good job, Dad! If your child wants to continue to believe, even after you've told her the "truth," by all means allow it, as this family did.

Maintaining Myths Past Readiness

"My son is now nine and a half, and I'm quite sure he was ready to hear about the myths awhile back. But we didn't know how to present it to him, so every time he asked, we responded by saying 'Of course there's a Santa (or Tooth Fairy, or Easter Bunny)!' Now I think he's maintaining the myth for us, instead of the other way around."

Some parents steadfastly stick to the myths because it's difficult to know exactly when their child is ready to hear the truth. Other parents may continue to maintain the existence of Santa or the Tooth Fairy because they are not ready to let their children give them up. After all, these characters can be just as much fun for most parents as they are for the children. So if you find yourself in this position, don't rush out now and try to correct it. But do listen closely for the next time your child asks, and respond appropriately at that point.

Chapter 16
All About the "Birds and Bees"

Preschoolers vs. Elementary School Children

Preschoolers usually are not looking for complicated answers when they ask about reproduction. In fact, many times when preschoolers ask Mom or Dad "Where did I come from?" and begin to hear the answer about sperm and eggs and assorted body parts, they look puzzled and reply along the lines of "But Sally came from St. Vincent's Hospital. What hospital did I come from?"

By the time your child is in elementary school, however, he's ready for more detailed information. Charles Schaefer, Ph.D., indicates that if your child hasn't actually asked you about sex by the time he's seven, it's quite possible that he has already sought out the information from a friend. This information may be erroneous, however.

One classic story involves a woman who told her son that he could tell his classmates at school that she was going to have a baby. Week after week, he'd tell the class that his mother was going to have a baby. Finally he came back to his mother and asked, "Mom, where is the baby, anyway?" She replied, "It's in my tummy." With that, at the next school meeting, he told the class, "Forget the baby, my mother ate it."

Whether erroneous information is a result of a misunder-
standing or because the child sought it out from friends who may
have distorted it, it's important that parents be prepared both to
initiate conversation regarding reproduction and to answer questions about it.

Answering Questions About Sex

In general, the rule of thumb is to answer only the question you've
been asked. State your answer clearly, simply, and using the
proper terminology. Be honest and direct, and if you don't know
the answer, offer to look it up. If you're not entirely sure what
question your child is asking, ask her to clarify.

**"My daughter came home from school one day and asked where
she came from. I wasn't sure if she was asking about sex or about
citizenship, so I said 'I'm not sure what you're asking. Can you
find a different way to phrase your question, or a way to explain
it?' Her answer was 'Well, Jessie came from her mommy's tummy,
but Sally's adopted. Where did I come from?' When I had that
information, it was easier to answer with 'I'm your biological
mother, so you grew in my uterus.' That seemed to satisfy her."**

This mother did a good job. She clarified the question her daughter was asking, gave a short, accurate answer and used the proper
term, "uterus," rather than "tummy." Because her daughter was
satisfied, it wasn't necessary for her to elaborate further.

Sometimes Things Don't Unfold Exactly the Way You'd Expect

**"Well, that's just fine if your child is satisfied. But sometimes they
keep asking more and more questions and never let up. My
daughter and I were on the public bus and she was playing with
a plastic octopus. She wanted me to look at it and, in a very loud**

voice, she said, 'Look, Mommy, it has eight testicles.' I tried to correct her and told her the word was 'tentacles.' So she asked me, "Well, what are testicles?" I told her that testicles are the sacks that hang behind a man's penis. She was very puzzled and asked me what testicles are for. I plowed ahead and explained that they're the place where the man's sperm is made. Of course, that led to 'What's sperm?'

"I told her that sperm combines with the egg in the woman's body to make a baby. My daughter's jaw dropped. 'How does it get in there?' At this point I realized that we were in deep, and even though it was in public, she was clearly fascinated now and I would have to finish what I'd started. So I told her that sperm gets in there when the man puts his penis in the woman's vagina. The sperm travels through the penis and into the woman's uterus where it meets the egg. What was kind of funny was that my daughter was clearly flabbergasted and amazed at this news because her next comment was 'And that makes a *baby*?' I affirmed that it did indeed 'make a baby.' She was quiet for a minute, and then her face changed. Her eyes got wide, and she slowly turned to look at me. 'You mean *Daddy* did that to *you*!?' "

It's not uncommon for children to take much of the information about the reproductive act in stride and feel curious or even amazed. It's like any other scientific information—factual, not personal. The shock, and unfortunately sometimes dismay, may come when they recognize that the most important people in their lives are involved. If your child appears angry or extraordinarily upset by the news that you and your spouse have sex, it's important to tell her that sex is also called "making love," and that it's a pleasurable and loving act that many grown-ups enjoy. This mother continued casually, which was appropriate, given that her daughter seemed surprised but not unduly upset.

"'Well, yes, honey, that's why we have you.' I could tell that she was less happy with this development, because her eyes narrowed and she looked at me accusingly. 'How come I didn't see it?' she wanted to know. So I told her that it was something grown-ups do in private and that no one gets to see. Well, then, she wanted to know how many times we'd done it. I have to tell you that it was too much for me. I just couldn't quite bring myself to discuss the frequency of sex with her, so I replied, 'It only takes once to make a baby.' "

Bravo! As public and unconventional as this conversation was, Mom did a great job handling it. She responded honestly to each question without giving her daughter too much information, and in spite of it taking place in a very public spot, she showed only very minor discomfort. Likewise, it was completely unnecessary for her to discuss how many times she and her husband had sex. There are things that are private, and she didn't answer untruthfully. If her daughter had pressed her about the point she could also have said "That's private information."

What Happens When Your Child Never Asks?

"I wish my son *would* ask me—I wouldn't even care if it was on the bus at this point! Two years ago, I thought that he would have questions, especially since I was pregnant with his brother. He knew that I was going to have a baby, but never seemed curious about how it got in there to begin with. Now he's eight and I'm not quite sure how to handle the whole thing."

Sometimes our children don't ask the questions that, ultimately, they need to know. While this may happen because they truly aren't curious, most often it's because they've either gotten the information elsewhere, or somehow have received the message that it's forbidden or wrong to talk about. Unfortunately, sometimes even with the best intentions, parents unintentionally send the message that the topic is uncomfortable.

"I remember when I was about eight years old, and I was in the bathroom with my mother. She was changing her tampon (surreptitiously, of course), but I noticed the string. I pointed it out to her, and she was *so* uncomfortable! Even though she told me what it was, I really got the sense that it was a terribly embarrassing subject. The result was that for years I was mortified to go to the store to buy tampons—I used to make my father get them. It spread to other things as well—for example, even the word 'bra' would make me cringe. I really don't want to do that to my kids."

Creating a Comfortable Atmosphere

Whenever the question of discussing sex comes up in a group, I always can tell who's not comfortable with the topic. Men squirm in their seats, women drop their eyes, people begin to use euphemisms like "tushie" and "down there." With this much discomfort on the part of the adults, children are going to pick up the message that the topics of reproduction, sex, masturbation, and the like are embarrassing and off limits. The problem with creating topics that are completely off limits in the family is that children often wind up feeling that "I'd better be careful when talking with Mom or Dad, some things aren't allowed." With this beginning, children become naturally cautious about bringing up new topics, because they're not sure which ones are okay and which are not. Eventually, often it's easier to view Mom or Dad as generally unapproachable and shut down communication altogether.

Creating a comfortable atmosphere within which your child can communicate questions and concerns requires that you feel comfortable with the topic yourself. This isn't always easy. Depending on your level of discomfort, it may require that you practice using the proper vocabulary with another adult to desensitize yourself or increase your confidence. Try this test: Practice saying these words out loud.

penis
vagina
intercourse
uterus
testicles
nipples
sperm
erection
masturbation
ejaculation

Did you blush, squirm, or stutter when you said them? How about when you just read them to yourself? Keep practicing. This will help you be more comfortable in front of your children.

When I told my seven-year-old daughter that I was writing this chapter about sex, she said some wise words that it may help you to remember. She said, "You know, it's really no big deal. If you hadn't had sex, you wouldn't have had me."

Nudity

Part of creating comfort in your home involves how you handle nudity. Many parents feel comfortable with nudity (their own and their child's) for a number of years. At some point, however, both parent and child may feel the need for privacy.

"My six-year-old daughter used to run around naked all the time. We jokingly referred to her as 'our little nudist.' All of a sudden, she's decided that she wants 'her privacy.' She shuts the bathroom door, dresses and undresses in the privacy of her own room, and prefers to bathe by herself."

"Well, my son's just the opposite. He's nine and still runs around in front of the family with no clothes on. He likes having us chat

with him during his bath and never shuts the bathroom door, except when company is around."

Most children feel the need for privacy sometime during the elementary school years, but the age at which this happens varies widely. Respecting your child's wishes about his privacy while maintaining a casual attitude is best. When your child begins to request privacy, a simple statement along the lines of "Okay, everyone needs privacy sometimes" works well. It communicates respect and understanding, without sending the message that bodies are something to be ashamed of.

Parental Nudity

"My husband and I have always taken a casual attitude about our own nudity. What age should my children be when we begin to wear robes or dress without letting them come in our bedroom?"

I'm frequently asked when parents should begin to worry about being nude in front of their children. Truthfully, I think the age of your child has less to do with when you should "cover up" than what your attitude about nudity is.

"I remember walking in on my father when I was about nine. He had his back turned toward me, but he was totally nude. He must have heard me or sensed I was there, because he literally scrambled to cover up. I backed out and never made the mistake of entering without knocking again. I'm sure that there were other incidents that contributed, but I definitely got the distinct impression that the body was shameful and should be covered."

Plenty of parents choose early on in their children's lives to have privacy. A casual attitude will communicate that this is a matter of choice rather than embarrassment. Likewise, some parents feel completely comfortable walking around nude throughout their children's elementary school years. Regardless of your choice, it's important to communicate to your child that the human body is natural, beautiful, and deserving of respect.

When You Just Can't Get Comfortable

Sometimes our inhibitions are so strong because of the way we were raised that it's difficult to get comfortable with the topic of sexuality. Sometimes we need to rely on others to do the talking. Buying a book and sitting with your child when he reads it or having your spouse read it to him is better than making the topic off limits altogether or having him learn from his friends. You also can share your feelings of discomfort with your child by saying something like "This is a little hard for me to talk about, because when I was growing up my parents sent me the message that it was uncomfortable. But this is an extremely important subject for children and their parents to discuss, and I want you to feel as if you can always come to me if you have questions about it."

When Your Child Walks In on You
and Your Partner

"I have something to say," one man began hesitantly. "I'm really at a loss. You see, the other night, my wife and I were making love, and my daughter walked in on us. I mean, we were right in the middle of everything, and there was no way to disguise it. She stood there for a minute and then she ran out. We wanted to talk to her about it, but she closed her door and refused to speak to us. None of us has brought it up since. It's been a couple of days, and everyone is acting like things are normal, but I feel kind of weird about it."

As discreet as we may be about our sex lives, and as diligent as we may be about locking our bedroom door during sex (and yes, you should lock your door), mistakes happen. This is obviously not the ideal way for a child to find out about this loving and pleasurable act, especially since many children are likely to misinterpret the noises they hear or the movement they see as aggressive or violent. It's important to follow up with your child if she walks in on you, even if she's not ready to listen immediately afterward.

You can begin by saying that you know she came into the room the other night, and ask if she has any questions about what she saw. Some children will speak up and ask, others may still be hesitant. Regardless, you must take the initiative and explain that you were making love, which also means that you were having sex. Tell her that it's something adults do in private because they love each other a great deal and that it doesn't hurt or feel uncomfortable. Ask one more time if she has any questions, then leave it. And do be sure that your door is locked next time.

What About Masturbation?

Masturbation is a very natural part of your child's development. Children often begin touching themselves as infants and toddlers because it feels good. The pleasant sensation they get from masturbation doesn't disappear during the elementary school years, though the frequency of masturbation may diminish because their interests are diverted during this period. Regardless of children's ages, it is normal for them to touch their genitals at least occasionally. If this should occur in front of you, it's appropriate to say "I know it feels good to touch your penis/vagina/vulva, and touching yourself is fine. It's a private activity, though, so you may touch yourself when you're alone, but not with other people."

Playing "Doctor"

Sometimes your child's natural curiosity will lead him to tell another child "If you show me yours, I'll show you mine." Sometimes this show-and-tell leads to "playing doctor," with the children alternating doctor and patient roles and actually touching each other's bodies. While this is also normal, it's important to tell your child that it's inappropriate to touch another person or allow another person to touch him, even in play. Tell him that if he's curious about how other people look, you'll show him photographs or pictures in a book. He only has to ask.

Talking to Your Child about Sexual Abuse

It's unfortunate that our children have to be warned about potential abuse. I haven't met a parent yet who hasn't wished that things were easier or that such warnings didn't need to occur. But not warning our children won't make them less vulnerable, and it won't change reality. Children who aren't forewarned are more at risk than children who not only have knowledge about the potential for abuse but are armed with techniques to handle it.

It begins with knowing what sexual abuse is.

"My two-year-old son was angry at his older sister. He reached up, grabbed her nipple, and pinched her. I know that he wasn't intentionally aiming there, but I also knew that she didn't need to be involved in a debate about 'intent.' My wife immediately withdrew my son from the room, and we sat down with my daughter, who was crying. We were very serious about telling her that it was unacceptable for anyone—even her own brother—to touch or hurt her breasts or her genitals. Those were her own private places, and no one was allowed to touch or hurt her there. We took the opportunity to talk about how sometimes grown-ups do

things that are wrong, and if anyone—even a grown-up—ever tried to touch her or did touch her or hurt her, she should come and tell us. We also said that sometimes the person who does those things tries to convince the child that she shouldn't tell. That sometimes the person will say things like 'I'll hurt you if you tell,' or 'I'll kill your mommy or daddy if you tell,' but those would be lies. They would never be able to hurt us, and we'd make very sure that they didn't hurt her again. The most important thing is to come to us so that we can help. We also said we would never, ever be angry with her for telling us."

Just knowing what abuse is isn't enough, however. Our children also must have tools to help them handle the situation when they're faced with it. This father went on:

"We also told our daughter that if anyone—again, including her little brother—tried to touch or hurt her, she should scream 'No!' and push them away or run. Then we had her role play. I asked her to push me and scream 'No.' She was really reluctant to do this, but I figured that if she didn't feel comfortable with me, how would she feel with someone else? Eventually, she screamed loud enough and pushed me hard enough."

When we not only educate and inform our children but also give them techniques and then role play those techniques with them as this family did, we empower our children to handle these difficult situations. Boys as well as girls should be informed about sexual abuse and harassment. And remember that these are not one-time discussions but ones that we should have regularly with our children so that they will retain the information.

Answering Questions About Homosexuality

"My son, who was six at the time, my wife and I were in Central Park in New York when the Gay Pride Parade was in full swing.

As we were leaving the park for the afternoon, a lot of the parade participants were coming in. I wasn't quite sure how to explain to my son why men were holding hands with and kissing other men, and why the women were doing the same."

While most parents won't be faced with being in New York City during a Gay Pride Parade, homosexuality is a misunderstood and often ignored topic in sex education. I sincerely believe that homosexuality should be treated in the same way as heterosexuality. Respond to your child's questions simply and age appropriately. Be honest and straightforward. If this father's son had asked, Dad could have said that sometimes men fall in love and want long-term relationships with other men instead of women and vice versa.

"My daughter asked about homosexuality and we told her that very thing, but then she wanted to know how two men or two women make babies."

In this case, you could simply tell your daughter that two men can't make a baby together, nor can two women. But sometimes people who are homosexual will adopt a baby when they want one.

Talking to Your Child About Puberty

Because of better health and nutrition, many children are maturing earlier than they used to. Girls are likely to experience the onset of puberty between the ages of nine and eleven, boys are likely to reach puberty slightly later—between eleven and fourteen. This means that we must prepare our children during the elementary school years so that they are not bewildered by the physical and psychological changes they will experience.

Preparing Your Daughter

"I noticed that my daughter was really moody and irritable. She's only nine and a half, so I figured it was just a phase. But the other day, when she was taking her bath, I noticed that she's starting to get pubic hair. You don't think that she's already hitting puberty, do you?"

While a medical doctor is the most qualified to ascertain the onset of puberty in any individual child, it's true that pubic hair, hair under the arms, an increase in breast size, and sometimes a widening of the hips are the first sign that puberty is beginning. If you haven't talked to your daughter about puberty by age nine, whether these signs are present or not, it's time to do so. After the secondary characteristics appear, menstruation follows. When you discuss puberty with your daughter, you should include the following topics:

- Physical changes in her body, including the development of breasts, pubic and underarm hair, a widening of her hips, and menstruation.
- Possible emotional changes, including moodiness, irritability, tenseness, tiredness, inexplicable sadness or anger. Sexual desires and thoughts may begin at this time as well.
- Menstruation, which is also called "getting your period." Include a discussion of the physical process of menstruation, how often a woman menstruates, and how to use sanitary napkins or tampons. Be sure to tell your daughter that when she gets her period for the first time, the flow of blood will be relatively slow. If it happens at school, she should go to the school nurse. Explain that sometimes women feel minor discomfort (or cramps), but that they usually go away after the first day or two.

Puberty should be lauded as a special time for your daughter, because it is now that she becomes a woman. At the same time, it's important to know that your daughter may have very mixed feelings about the changes in her body and feelings, and overdoing it may make her feel misunderstood by you.

Preparing Your Son

The onset of puberty for our sons will, in general, occur later than it does for our daughters. Still, preparation is the name of the game. Included in your discussion should be the following topics:

- Physical changes, including an enlargement of the scrotum and penis, the development of pubic, underarm, chest and facial hair, and a deepening of the voice. Following these changes by about a year is the ability to produce and ejaculate sperm.
- "Wet dreams," which are a normal part of our sons' development. You should emphasize that there is no need to worry if his pajamas or sheets are wet in the morning. More frequent erections are also to be expected.
- Psychological changes, including sexual desires and thoughts. Boys also may experience changes in mood, feelings of confusion, worry, sadness, or anger. While these mood changes may not seem as extreme as those our daughters experience, they are no less important and should be discussed.

About AIDS and Other Sexually Transmitted Diseases

While elementary school may seem young to begin talking to your child about AIDS and other STDs (sexually transmitted diseases), the reality is that between the media and what your child will hear in school, it's likely that even if you fail to bring up the subject, your child will ask you about it. Sadly, many young children growing up today will personally know someone who dies of AIDS. In the past few years I've known of at least three elementary school children who have lost close relatives to this disease—two lost their mothers, one lost an uncle who lived in his home. Talking openly about both AIDS and STDs helps educate, diminish unreasonable fears, and, it is hoped, prevent mistakes that may have life-threatening consequences.

"We were on the subway and there was a poster about AIDS. There were all kinds of people represented, some with babies on their laps. My daughter wanted to know what it meant and were all those people sick. I told her that yes, they were sick, that they had a disease called AIDS. She wanted to know how you got AIDS, so I explained that you could contract the disease in a number of ways—the main ways are by using intravenous drugs and by having unprotected sex. She asked if the baby in the photo had AIDS too. I replied that babies could also get AIDS, but not the same way that adults do. I suddenly realized that this was actually more complicated than boiling it down to intravenous drug use and unprotected sex. I also remembered a friend who contracted AIDS during a blood transfusion. How could I sort through all that for my daughter, if I was having trouble sorting it through for myself?"

The first step in talking to your child requires that you have accurate information yourself. Then, as with any other subject, answer your child's questions simply and age appropriately.

In addition, prioritize the information you give your child. While she needs to know that contracting AIDS isn't always the person's fault (i.e., when it's transmitted through a blood transfusion, or when a baby has AIDS), the usefulness of that information is negligible for the elementary school child. More important is for her to hear about the areas in which she has some control, where her future choices will affect her life. Remember, too, that it's not necessary to cram all the information into one discussion. Fortunately, for most elementary school children, we have time so that our discussion of STDs can be ongoing.

Communicating Values

It is never too early to begin communicating your values about sex to your children. In her book *Reviving Ophelia*, which talks primarily about adolescent girls but contains important messages for parents of both boys and girls, Mary Pipher, Ph.D, says "Guess Jeans, Madonna, and 2 Live Crew are not shy about communicating their sexual values. You must present [your children] with your message."

We live in a confusing society. Children are deluged with sexual imagery and messages. They are told that sex is something you should wait until you're older to have. Yet almost all of what they see not only connects sex with extreme youth but even mixes it in with violence. Just today I passed a movie poster where a gun-toting older man stood with a voluptuous young blonde in an unbearably short tight outfit hanging on his shoulder. Advertisements for blue jeans and other clothing show scantily clad young women and men draped all over each other. The messages to our impressionable elementary school children are mixed and extreme. It's crucial that you communicate your values to your children in ways that they can absorb and retain.

Using Television, Media, and Print to Help You Communicate Values

Unfortunately, there's no way to get rid of the images our children will see throughout their elementary school years. And traditional "lecturing" about values probably will get you nowhere. I propose that instead of allowing the images of the media to enter your child unfiltered, you use them as a teaching tool. Because children are fascinated with the world around them, having a discussion about what they see and what they think it means often provides parents with an opportunity to instill values.

"We were watching my son's favorite TV program. It has a group of kids on it that are friends. At the first commercial, I asked him, 'Why do you think all those kids are friends? Do you think it's because of the way they look, or do you think the boys and girls are interested in each other, or what?' He thought for a minute, and then said, 'I think it's because they have something in common. They all like to tell stories, and that brings them together.' 'What do you think would happen if one of them decided that the others had to look a certain way or he wouldn't stay their friend?' My son thought again, then said, 'I think that would be dumb, because it's not looks that matter, but what's inside the person. They probably wouldn't be friends with him if he changed like that.' "

Through skillfully asking questions about the nature of friendship, this parent was able to encourage her son to think about the values that people hold when forming relationships. Similar questions can help children understand what movie, commercials, and television are "selling" us in terms of ideas and values.

"A bus went by the other day, and it had one of those advertisements on it where the girl has an open shirt with her bra showing, and her jeans are unzipped and open to display the name brand of her underwear. Next to her stood a young man, also partially clad, with his arm around her. His jeans were unzipped too. So I pointed it out to my daughter and asked her what she thought it was selling. At first she shrugged and said, 'Underwear, or maybe jeans.' I probed a little deeper and said,

'What do you think the message is about the product?' Her head tilted and she frowned. 'Well, it looks like if you wear that stuff, you'll get a boyfriend or girlfriend.' Bingo! So I said, 'How old do you think those kids are?' 'Probably about twelve,' she said. 'And what do you think of them being undressed like that in front of each other?' I continued. 'I'd be embarrassed!' she said. So I took the opportunity to slip a little lesson in. 'Yeah, I think maybe it's a little young for them to be that serious. And I kind of resent it that the people who made the advertisement are trying to sell young people things in that way. I think another message is that it's okay to do the stuff you see up there, like being undressed in front of your boyfriend when you're only twelve.' Much to my delight, she replied, 'And it's not okay, you should be much older.' "

Remember that one of the most effective teaching tools you have is open-ended questions. When children respond to your queries with answers in their own words, it helps them internalize the values more thoroughly than your preaching would.

What If My Child Gives the "Wrong Answer"?

"I love this idea!" one father responded. "But I'm afraid my child will say yes, it's okay for them to be undressed in front of each other, or yes, it's okay for them to look as if they're going to have sex in the next five minutes."

That could happen. If your child should respond differently from the values that you would like him to hold, I recommend that first you ask him a few more questions, such as 'What do you mean?' 'What about that do you think is okay or right?' Often children don't mean exactly what they say, and perhaps with a little more questioning, your child will divulge that he thinks it's okay for the boy to have his arm around the girl, for example.

If your questioning fails to uncover any new information, however, I recommend Mary Pipher's "sandwich technique" for giving feedback: Start with a positive statement, slip in your values, end with a positive statement. It might sound something like this: "I admire that you've thought about this. I feel concerned when I see advertisements like that because sexuality and nudity are meaningful to loving couples and those advertisements make them seem trivial. Thank you for sharing your opinion with me even though we disagree." This technique values your child's developing opinions and leaves the lines of communication open for further discussion.

Don't Be Alarmed

Finally, it's important not to become too alarmed if your child speaks values vastly different from your own. The values he holds in elementary school will develop and change in fundamental ways before he reaches adulthood, and should be treated as stepping-stones toward the values you'd like for him to hold eventually. Ask open-ended questions, use the sandwich technique, and help him feel comfortable seeking information from you about his body and his sexuality, and you'll stand a good chance of instilling within him the values you hold dear.

In Conclusion

One of the most delightful experiences I have in my workshops is when I sense that children are comfortable not only with their bodies but in communicating with their parents as well.

One seven-year-old girl came home from school and said to her mother, "I had the greatest day at school today. Sarah and I were laughing and laughing and we just couldn't stop. Mommy, I laughed so hard my vagina wiggled."

This child is growing up healthy, with a good attitude about her body. She's both informed and comfortable with the information she has. Perhaps most important, she's growing up trusting her parents to be there to discuss any and all of the questions, concerns, and even traumas she may have in the future.

Chapter 17

About You

If you've gotten to this chapter in the book, you've had an opportunity to contemplate and, it is hoped, even put to use the tools and techniques that will make you a more effective parent, will improve your relationship with your elementary school child, and will pave the way for a less turbulent adolescence. Perhaps you've used some of the tools with success, and if so, congratulations! It's also possible that some of the tools have been difficult to implement; maybe you've read them, thought they'd be helpful, but in your rush to get the kids off to school that morning, you threw the book down and it got lost under a pile of bills. Or maybe you just felt too tired and irritable that day to try something new, and yelling was easier and seemed to work—after all, the kids *did* do what you asked, albeit resentfully.

A book about child rearing wouldn't be completely honest unless it acknowledged that sometimes it's difficult to put into practice the things we've learned. I think the difficulty arises from some things that stand in the way of our being more effective, loving parents. I hope that reflecting on these issues within this chapter will help you more successfully use the tools contained herein.

Our Parents' Voices

Perhaps the most formidable obstacle that stands in our way as parents is our personal history. By that I mean the way we were raised by our own parents or guardians. Time and again, people come into my workshops and when asked why they're taking a parenting course, they say, "Because I don't want to do it the way my parents did." Yet they find themselves confused and bewildered, because in spite of their best intentions, they hear the very things their parents said to them coming out of their own mouths when they talk to their own children. Why is that? Like it or not, the way our parents raised us is deeply ingrained in our subconscious. So deeply, in fact, that the memories may never even surface. When we are stressed or frustrated or tired, our brain automatically draws upon those hidden memories of the way we were raised, particularly if we have not learned an alternative way of disciplining or communicating. Hence, we hear our mother or father's voice coming out of our mouth, yelling, punishing, belittling, or any one of a number of things we told ourselves we'd never do or say. Afterward we may even go a step further and justify our behavior because we really feel a little guilty. We may say to ourselves "Oh well, I turned out okay, so my kids will too." And in justification, we perpetuate the cycle.

Parenting today is a difficult task—more difficult than the one our parents faced. The widespread use of television, the availability of alcohol and drugs—these are among the things that make parenting today different and more difficult for us than it was for our parents. Yet even with this knowledge, even knowing that the "old" ways won't do, even with our best intentions not to duplicate the parenting we had, we sometimes continue to rely on "instinct" and/or reacting the way our parents did and hoping that these old ways will get us (and our children) through it.

The Time Factor

So it's not just our personal history that keeps us stuck in old molds, because even when we're aware of the need to change and have the desire to do so, often we do not. Perhaps another thing that stands in the way of becoming the parents we'd like to be is time. There never seems to be enough of it. Between our children's social and school calendars, our work (either in the home or out of it), our social and personal agendas, there seems to be very little time left to devote to learning the parenting skills we recognize as potentially beneficial. The lack of time in our lives coupled with our personal history and the ease with which we slip automatically into whatever parenting style our parents used sometimes make it just seem easier to give up and give in to yelling or other ineffective methods of discipline and "communication." One father said to me after a two-hour workshop I gave, "All this is great. It's great as we sit here and listen with no distractions. It's fine in theory. But I work all day. I come home tired. And when my son starts in, I just don't have the patience. I can't do this when I'm tired."

The Stress Factor

He's right. When we're stressed, overworked, tired . . . these are the times that it's the most difficult to be an effective and loving parent. It's like strengthening a muscle that you rarely or never use. When you go to the gym for the first time, you can't expect to be able to lift a 200-pound weight. You have to build up to it. You have to start with a one-pound weight the first time. And after that first time at the gym, you'll probably be sore and tired. You may have even skipped some of the exercises or machines that you know you should use to get stronger. Maybe you'll even avoid the gym for a week. But the second time around, you might be able to lift the two-pound weight. You're building muscle. In order to have a healthy body, you have to exercise muscles you may have never used before and build up to using them efficiently and effectively. Just like a healthy body, a healthy family requires that you start with small things, make the effort, and build up to the big issues. Once learned, parenting skills are simply muscles that must be put to work in order to become stronger.

Overcoming the Obstacles

So what are some things you can do in order to develop a stronger, healthier parenting style? Further, what can you do if you find yourself slipping into old patterns, despite your best intentions?

One of the best things you can do for yourself and for your children is to sign up for a parenting workshop. Workshops provide the support you need because they give you contact with a group of parents who are all struggling with the same issues and the application of the same techniques. In addition, when the techniques don't work in the way you expect them to, you have the help of an instructor to guide you through them and increase your chances of success. Think of it like going to the gym with a buddy or even a personal trainer. You're more likely not only to go to the gym if someone is with you, but also to work harder once you're there.

Another thing you can do is to keep reading. You can't learn too much about your important job as a parent. And sometimes simply hearing the same things you already know said in a different way can give you a different perspective that might make overcoming some of the obstacles that stand in your way easier.

In addition, rather than complaining that there's not enough time, be proactive and take the time, both to learn and to practice skills. Parenting is learned, not instinctual, and if you take the time now, I can guarantee it will save you time in the future because your relationship with your child will be healthier and therefore have less conflict.

It's also important that you not expect to be perfect the first time. Using the analogy of the gym once again, you can't expect to lift 200-pound weights when you're tired and stressed. It takes time to build muscle, and you need to exercise your skills when you're rested. Start small and build to big issues. Practice when you're not stressed, and eventually it will carry over to the parts of your day when you are tired. If you make some mistakes, forgive yourself. You are, after all, a human being, both fallible and forgivable. In forgiving yourself, you open the door that will allow you to learn from your mistakes rather than justifying and perhaps therefore repeating them.

Finally, take care of yourself. Because we lapse mostly when we're tired and stressed, our taking care of ourselves by exercising, eating properly, and getting enough rest can only benefit all the members of our families. The added benefit is that by doing so, you will teach your children that taking care of themselves is valuable as well.

As you go forward in the great adventure of raising your children, remember that it is the most important job you'll ever hold. If you train for it and take it seriously, as you would a job that pays seven figures, you will be wealthy indeed.

Good luck!

Bibliography

Covey, Steven. *The 7 Habits of Highly Effective People.* New York: Simon & Schuster, 1989.

Elium, Jeanne, and Don Elium. *Raising a Daughter:* Berkeley, California: Celestial Arts, 1994.

The Gesell Institute Series: Your One-Year-Old, Your Two-Year-Old . . . (continues through adolescence). New York: Harper & Row.

Ginott, Haim. *Between Parent & Child.* New York: Avon Books, 1956.

Goleman, Daniel. *Emotional Intelligence.* New York: Bantam Books, 1995.

Hirschmann, Jane, and Lela Zaphiropoulos. *Preventing Childhood Eating Problems.* Carlsbad, California: Gurze Books, 1993.

Ilg, Frances, Louise Bates Ames, and Sidney M. Baker. *Child Behavior.* New York: Harper & Row, 1981.

Landreth, Garry. *Play Therapy: The Art of the Relationship.* Accelerated Development, 1991.

Magid, Ken, and Carole A. McKelvey. *High Risk: Children Without a Conscience.* New York: Bantam Books, 1987.

Marston, Stephanie. *The Magic of Encouragement.* New York: Penguin Books, 1987.

Pipher, Mary. *Reviving Ophelia: Saving the Selves of Adolescent Girls.* New York: Putnam Publishing Group, 1994.

Popkin, Michael. *Active Parenting.* San Francisco: Harper & Row, 1987.

Ross, Julie A. *Practical Parenting for the 21st Century.* New York: Excalibur Publishing, 1993.

Satter, Ellyn. *How to Get Your Kid to Eat . . . But Not Too Much.* Palo Alto, California: Bull Publishing, 1987.

Schaefer, Charles. *How to Talk to Your Children About Really Important Things.* New York: Harper & Row, 1984.

Parenting Horizons is a company, located in New York City, that offers workshops for parents, teachers, and children. It also offers private counseling services. Phone number: (212) 765-2377.